Dedication

To my husband, who always saw my potential in writing this book and supported me unwaveringly through the whole process. From the moment you met me you believed in me, so much that I remembered to once again believe in myself. Thank you so much for that! The love I feel with you gives me the strength and inspiration to help others know they can feel this, too.

To my beautiful mother, who has always had my back and supported my thinking even when it was way outside the box. Thank you for that. You get me, and I get you. I love that! I cherish our connection. You are one of my biggest inspirations.

≈ Chapters ≈

THE PATH TO
HIGHER
CONSCIOUSNESS

Creating and Healing Our Lives By Awakening to Our Greater Reality

DAVID T HOWARD PHD

PocketStone Publishing Powell, Ohio

Printed in the United States of America.

Editor: Heather Doyle Fraser www.cmcollab.com

Copyeditor: Hope Madden

Cover Design: Alex Allerandre

Interior Design and Layout: WinZoe Creations transcendentlifestyle.com

Proofreader: Hope Madden

Author Headshots: Jessica Lowman www.jesslowmanphotography.com

ISBN: 978-1-7341566-9-0

Important Note: The information provided in this book is designed to provide helpful information on the subjects discussed. This book is not meant to be used, nor should it be used, to diagnose or treat any medical or psychological condition. For diagnosis or treatment of any medical or psychological problem, consult your own physician. The publisher and author are not responsible for any specific health or psychological needs that may require medical supervision and are not liable for any damages or negative consequences from any treatment, action, application or preparation, to any person reading or following the information in this book. Our views and rights are the same: You are responsible for your own choices, actions, and results.

≈ Exercises ≈

Exercises

Chapter 1

Introduction

The goal of this book is to help you realize the existence of a Source that is available to all of us to help create and heal our lives. This Source does not tell us how to live, rather it supports how we live through loving guidance. We have free will to choose how we perceive our physical lives, but non-belief and disbelief in a non-physical existence does not take away from the truth that we are all supported and loved by Source.

It takes our own conscious effort to move beyond the limitations we put on our thinking and awaken to this greater truth, but the benefit in doing so is tremendous. Allowing Source into our minds and lives brings forth the loving support, guidance and wellbeing it consists of. The problem is that most of us are not raised to believe we are always loved and supported by God. These limiting beliefs make it difficult to form a healthy relationship with the non-physical Source of our existence. Most of us seek answers and truths that could lead to a loving relationship with Source, yet truth can be hard to decipher when so many powerful beliefs have been layered onto what we currently perceive as God. We are experiencing beliefs that stem back hundreds if not thousands of years, beliefs that may not serve us today when it comes to believing in ourselves as powerful, worthy and loved by God.

Many of the traditions created around our spiritual beliefs are beautiful and should be cherished, but if the core of our spiritual beliefs does not serve us, we need to try and see it from a higher perspective. From a higher perspective, we can begin to see the truth in beliefs that are loving and beneficial because we learn this is what our Source truly is. We also begin to recognize the untruths of human thoughts and motives that are injected into so many of our spiritual teachings — thoughts and motives that are out of alignment with our loving Source. True spiritual teachings espouse loving union and support; human ego thinking adds judgement, condemnation and the feeling of being separated from a higher power or God.

The goal of this book is not to change what you believe. Rather, it is a journey to strengthen your beliefs into something more positive and supportive by seeing them through a higher perspective, and not ego. The journey begins with a look at our current beliefs and perceptions. We must then learn how to think and feel in ways that are beneficial to our wellbeing and to creating the life we desire.

This book is a journey to strengthen your beliefs into

something more positive and supportive.

Beliefs

With so many beliefs and spiritual teachings at our fingertips, it can be difficult to understand what to believe — if anything at all. The major religions disagree with and even condemn each other, while new age spiritualists paint pictures of an afterlife that looks much like it does on Earth, only dreamier or more beautiful. With so much conflicting information, how do we discover for ourselves what is real and what is illusion or delusion? This was the question I asked myself when I actively began pursuing my spiritual journey.

I have always been on a spiritual path, as all of us are. But when I became more aware or awakened to my spiritual path, I opened my mind and began looking into many different teachings and experiences. This path led me to church, the internet, books, metaphysical schooling and to people who have the ability to sense the non-physical energies that are all around us. My journey of seeking spiritual answers and experiences has been interesting and fun, but mostly it has been enlightening. I chose activities that I was intuitively drawn to and used my discernment before accepting anything as my truth. Because I have an open mind, I was willing to attend, observe, participate and study so many different spiritual views and practices, and it was through this wide array of experiences that I was able to discover some basic truths in spiritual teachings.

The Basic Truths

One of the first truths that I discovered: we are all on our own paths, meaning we all perceive spiritual experiences and teachings differently depending on our mental perceptions. Another truth I discovered is that God, Source or the afterlife do not think with a human mind. Beliefs that state that God thinks about humans with human thoughts are actually only a result of human interpretations and perception. Any time we state our beliefs in absolutes or as a sole truth—and especially when we use words in our beliefs like *always*, *never*, *must* or *should*—it is a sure sign that this belief does not come from a higher power, but rather from our own minds and perceptions. To find truth in any spiritual teaching or experience, we sometimes need to override what we currently "know" by weeding out thoughts that are simply a result of the human experience.

Source and The Human Mind

"Source" will be mentioned frequently in this book because it is the word I used to explain where we spiritually come from and are part of. Others may refer to Source as God, higher self, higher mind, or even the Universe. For me, names are not what is important since they only help us to verbally describe that of which we speak, so Source is a word I use to describe the source of our existence. Source is a neutral word that does not come with any predetermined conditions, beliefs or resentments. This allows us to see spiritual ideas and concepts with a fresh, new perspective.

Source does not think with a human type of mind; it exists solely in a state of higher awareness. To better understand this concept, I will explain the various aspects of the human mind because it allows us to better understand how our thinking differs from the awareness of Source.

It is important to understand our ego thinking and how our minds are capable of more; we all have the ability to exist in a higher state of awareness beyond our ego thinking. It is through our higher conscious thoughts that we can align ourselves mentally with the higher consciousness of Source and receive the wisdom it offers. The higher consciousness of Source is not higher in the sense that it is better than a lower or lesser human mind; instead, it is just the best way to describe an awareness that exists beyond the human ego mind.

As humans, we have free will to either focus our ego minds on our differences and feel separate from one another and Source, or we can see our similarities through a higher conscious perspective and feel unified with others and Source. The choice is ours to make, but the reality is that we are all connected to each other and Source, and the illusion is that we are all separate.

Karma and Law of Attraction

I will bring up the topics of karma and the law of attraction in this book because, by removing our ego interpretations, these topics can be better understood. There is much ego focus on these spiritual laws and as a result, these laws may influence people to act in certain ways. I will show how karma, as it is seen today, is the perfect example of how our ego minds tend to color or alter spiritual teachings. As for the law of attraction, I will demonstrate that we do not choose to use it or not; it is always present and working whether we focus our awareness on it or not. With a better understanding of the concepts of karma and the law of attraction, we can see the true meaning behind them and decide if we want to recognize them in our lives or discard them.

It would be difficult to explain the higher consciousness of Source without inputting my own beliefs and experiences. I use these for inspiration and to show a different perspective. My beliefs are based on my own experiences along with my studies in metaphysics, which includes all religions but transcends the ego, which is injected into many of our spiritual teachings. I do make a sincere effort to present spiritual knowledge that is non-judgmental, inclusive and loving because that is what Source presents to me.

Who Am I?

Now that we know a little more about why I am writing this book, I want to tell you a little about who I am and how that relates to my coming to this work. In regards to my personality, I am fun-loving, outgoing, humorous, curious, intuitive, sensitive and open-minded to trying new things. I'm also a dog lover and a nature lover. In terms of my ego titles, I am a husband, a reverend, a metaphysical guide, a holistic coach, an author and a PhD. I have never really been a fan of titles because I just consider myself to be me, but I realize these are important badges in describing oneself to others. I did not seek ministerial status or to be a reverend; instead I sought spiritual answers. In my quest for this knowledge, and because of my accomplishments that came along with obtaining them, I was awarded the title of reverend and doctor. I do not get lost in ego or the predetermined personality society associates with a title, so it confuses people that I don't use the titles when introducing myself in person. I guess you might call me humble.

I consider myself to be passionate about life, and I am an avid believer in enjoying life. I don't believe in doing things I don't feel good about, but sometimes I need to do just that—like we all do—in order to help someone else. I became a spiritual seeker to find my own peace of mind in this world, which in turn led me to discover my own higher conscious awareness that exists beyond my ego thinking. Studying the human mental and spiritual existence has been my primary interest, and I keep an open mind to learning various concepts and views pertaining to it. Having an open mind is important because learning about many different beliefs and viewpoints has led me to evolve my own thinking and expand my awareness. This allows me to better understand why others believe the way they do and to see how their beliefs may not serve them. Because of my observations, I am able to better assist people in evolving.

I had so many questions about beliefs starting from a young age and I couldn't or wouldn't settle for the answer of "this is just how it is." Receiving this generic answer is what led me to study history, science, biology, psychology, philosophy, religion, law and eventually to get my ministerial PhD in metaphysics. It is through studying all of these subjects that I was able to connect the dots and see the historical thoughts, motives and actions that led to the beliefs many of us hold on to today. Along with schooling, I read many spiritual and self-help books and I took time to do work on myself and heal my own mind. When it comes to healing and growing spiritually, a person can only learn so much through reading; it takes clarifying the mind by practicing mindfulness, forgiveness, self-love and letting go of fear to truly heal and grow spiritually. The result of healing my own thinking required a greater sense of self-acceptance, self-love and awareness, which led me to become more intuitive and eventually to be able to receive spiritual insight from Source.

This process of receiving guidance and "knowing" from Source is very natural and fulfilling. Yet, it can be difficult to explain how Source is part of who we all are and because of this, we connect to Source when we move into our own higher conscious state of mind. One of the reasons I am writing this book is to try to explain just that. The mechanics behind receiving insight and wisdom is hard to comprehend for a human mind under the influence of ego, but when one understands that ultimately, we are all consciously connected beyond the ego, it is not difficult to see the possibility in this. Receiving insight and inspiration from Source is a natural process for all of us and we all do experience it; some of us just don't know it's happening, or we've shut ourselves off from recognizing it. An example would be when people think of creativity and inspiration as coming from physical brains when in reality it comes from the higher consciousness of Source.

I am quite intuitive, and also a sensitive person who picks up on subtle actions and energies from others. We are all intuitive, it's just that some of us were raised to acknowledge and develop our intuitions while others were taught to ignore it. I have worked to develop my intuition to a point where insight, ideas and inspiration come into my mind automatically. I receive inspiration and insight at random times, but especially while being in a peaceful state of mind. It can happen while I'm driving, having a conversation with someone and also upon waking or falling asleep. Because of this I keep a phone with a stylus pen, so I can write all of the insight and ideas down when they come to me; if I don't write the insights down, I usually forget them.

I will say this to anyone who wants to know who the sender of this wisdom and insight is: the wisdom we receive when we are in a higher conscious state of mind has been described to me as the conscious thoughts of God or Source coming into our own minds to mentally guide us and balance our energy. We cannot see this, just like we cannot see our own thoughts, but we can visualize it as a stream of white light energy. I am not any different from anyone else in receiving it, the only difference is that I chose to acknowledge that I can receive this energy and thus I allow myself to.

How to Use This Book

This book is written for you and designed to come to you where you are in your journey. For some, this may mean starting at the beginning and reading chronologically through from page one until the end. For others, this may mean listening to the inner voice that nudges you to start at a certain section. Whether you are called to start at the beginning or somewhere else, just start. What speaks to you? You can't do it wrong.

You will notice that each section contains exercises to help you on your journey. The exercises build on each other and are placed throughout the book to help you think more deeply about the topic being discussed. So, while this book allows you to start reading any section you are first drawn to, I do recommend starting the exercises from the beginning.

Once you engage with the exercises, make them a practice. Allow them to open you to possibility and contemplation. Some of the exercises are designed to help you reflect upon and think deeply about yourself and your life. If they do not feel comfortable or you simply are not interested in doing them, it is quite all right to skip over them for the time being, but consider coming back to complete them at a later time, when you are ready. It is my own belief that putting concepts to work in a practical way rather than just reading about them is the most effective way to expand our awareness and heal our minds. If you choose not to do the exercises, I highly recommend you at least give the manifesting exercise a try. It's a great way to put your mind to work in creating the life you desire.

The ultimate goal of the exercises is not just to lead you to becoming aware of your always-present connection with Source, but to help you realize we are capable of existing in a peaceful awareness beyond our ego thoughts. This peaceful awareness is where we align ourselves with the higher consciousness of Source. It is through this alignment that we can learn to heal our minds, assist in the healing of our bodies and receive creative insight and inspiration. The end result is that we learn to experience this world in a much more positive and enjoyable way!

Get yourself a journal or notebook (or use your computer) and make this journey a creative and fun one. Take your time with the exercises for there is no need to rush. I am sharing what works for me, but if there are other exercises you have learned that you want to do in conjunction with the ones I present, please do so. I sincerely hope my exercises will help inspire you to live life more fully, live life more passionately and manifest the life you desire.

The reward for examining one's own thoughts and feelings is the development of a stronger, more secure belief in oneself and the world, as well as a stronger connection to Source, a connection that transcends the fearful ego and allows one to live life with courage and passion.

Introduction to Higher Consciousness

We exist in a higher conscious state of mind when we let go of our thoughts of fear and doubt, allowing us to connect more fully with Source.

Day after day, we become so involved with keeping our schedules and taking care of our needs and the needs of others that we tend to forget there is so much more to who we are. We focus on what we can see and feel with our physical senses and we forget there are non-visible energies existing all around us and even in us. We can shut off our awareness of these unseen energies, but we can never shut these forces and energies out of our lives. If we were capable of shutting these energies out of our lives, we would no longer be alive because we thrive in a world that is dependent upon energies coming from Source.

Having a higher conscious perception allows us to see a reality that is made of energy and wisdom that exists beyond the temporary ego dramas of everyday human life. Source does not have an ego mind, that is why it exists in a eternal state of higher consciousness. Humans have the experience of an ego mind, which is a state of mind separate from Source. Ego allows us to exist in lower conscious states of mind, which are associated with negative thoughts such as fear and hate. When we transcend our ego minds, we exist in our own positive and loving higher conscious state of mind that allows us to connect with the higher consciousness of Source.

Source provides the energy that keeps us alive and in a physical body. We are an aspect of Source's energy that chooses to experience physical life. The part of Source that wishes to *experience* life is what we call Spirit, but it is not separate from Source; it is still connected. The energy of the Soul is our *connection* to Source while we are in a physical existence. There always exists a greater, non-physical Source behind all of creation, and we connect with Source by becoming aware of our Souls' eternal connection and by mentally existing in our own higher conscious state of mind.

As humans, we see through our own eyes that we are separate from other physical things, but we do not have physical bodies to separate us in the non-physical realm. To comprehend our non-physical existence, we must look beyond what we see with our eyes and our ego thoughts, because neither exist in the non-physical realm.

Everything is connected in the non-physical realm. There is no separation; everything flows together to form the collective of Source.

It is true our Soul is never separate from Source, yet because of ego, our human mind has free will to believe it is separate. We can choose to exist in an ego state of mind that mentally separates us from the higher consciousness of Source, or we can exist in our own higher conscious state of mind, meaning that we transcend our ego thinking and align with the higher consciousness of Source.

Our Spirit—our aspect of Source wishing to have a physical experience—sets an intention for this physical experience, but how the ego experience plays out depends on each person's own free will and perceptions. For example, some people may be fortunate to be born into a loving family, but many of us are not. This experience is not the result of Source rewarding or punishing us; it is merely the result of the ego perception of the family and culture we are born into. We have free will to think and do as we please here on Earth—our actions are not controlled by the higher consciousness of Source—so if our families lead us to have a bad experience growing up, it is because our family is lost in ego. We are not being punished by past life karma or God.

Our human life is full of contrasts such as good and bad, happy and sad, pretty and ugly, light and dark, hate and love. These contrasts are so overwhelming that they can overshadow the oneness from which we come. The purpose of the human experience is up to each of us as individuals to perceive, and we have free will to focus on the positive or negative. For some, perhaps the contrasts of this world allow them, if they choose, to lose sight of or forget their true spiritual nature so they can immerse themselves in the relationships and interactions of ego life. While for others, life experiences may be a tool for them to awaken to their greater truth in this lifetime.

From what I have learned, knowledge of how to have a connection to the higher consciousness of Source is a common thread in our ancient human teachings. But the controlling and influential powers that got us to where we are today have flourished greatly by dismissing and suppressing this knowledge. Because we lost the knowledge of how to recognize our own connection to higher consciousness, we now turn to others to tell us how to believe. This has resulted in many spiritual middlemen—people gaining power over us by making us feel as though we need to go through them to connect to God. This can lead to human mental concepts being injected into teachings and ultimately controlling what and how we believe. When this power is abused by church or spiritual leaders, many people suffer and become confused, and as a result they may turn away from any type of belief at all.

Suffering and losing awareness of our true spiritual nature is not part of divine design; however, the human ego may choose to create a lost and miserable existence. This lost existence makes us susceptible to falling into lonely, depressed and even vengeful existences full of rage and hate.

Many of us also become afraid to express ourselves in ways we desire because perhaps our desire does not fit with the roles our culture assigns to our gender, or our culture looks down on a certain career path or hobby. The fear of being judged or alienated can turn many people away from what it is they really have a desire to do and be, and as a result they may instead choose to get lost in materialism and competition to feel worthy or recognized. Our obsession with "being someone special" can lead to a stressful life, and no matter how much a person has, no matter how many games they have won, it's all just a temporary physical existence under the influence of ego.

For example, our Western culture prizes being a celebrity, but when we look at many of the personal lives of "celebrities" we can see how many of them are suffering from exhaustion, relationship issues and substance abuse, perhaps as a result of their demanding careers and being in the spotlight. What may appear as a "special life" can actually be a lonely and tormented existence in which a person is expected to fit the brand they created rather than be their authentic selves.

People do not have to change who they are or change what they do to have a connection to Source. This connection already exists, but when you focus on strengthening this connection, something almost magical happens: you are actually able to enjoy life more fully because you better understand what life means, and why you are here. Receiving divine insight and wisdom from Source does not require someone to be quiet all the time, doing yoga poses or dressing like a guru. I consider myself a spiritually awakened person who receives wisdom from Source, yet I also like to wear designer clothes, go to parties, plan luxury vacations, be a jokester, and drink cocktails. I also can have a higher conscious mindset and connect with Source while working a corporate job, and so can anyone else.

In this life, no one needs a title, and no one needs to be on a mission, nor are we here to be tested or judged. We are merely here to have an individualized experience. How we choose to individually perceive this experience is up to each of us, and any one of us at any time can choose to see this life as a beautiful life worth living and live it up by enjoying every day. If all individuals were to choose this perception, this could temporarily be a more peaceful world. But with ego, we will always be led back into some type of conflict. Despite this inevitability, we each have a choice to fall prey to our egos or to try our best to rise above at least the negative aspects of it in each moment.

No matter what we believe or do, when our physical bodies die, our awareness moves into a nonphysical state, and it is then we finally realize that life was all about the experiences we had, not our material things, our careers or even our beliefs.

With the rampant dread, insecurities and anxiety many people of this world are experiencing, humanity needs people who are living modern lives—especially those raising families and working in the business world—to awaken and remember who and what we truly are.

People who work in business or have corporate jobs do not have to change what they do for a living to do this. Instead, if they continue doing the work toward awakening, then corporate environments and businesses will expand along with them into more compassionate and heart-centered places. The modern world would benefit greatly by having heart-centered, spiritually connected people working in the corporate world and also moving into government positions to inspire and lead.

This can't happen if everyone who wakes up to a higher conscious understanding goes to live off the grid or to work as a spiritual teacher and writer. Some of us need to be in the trenches of modern life, at least partly. Society focuses too much on changing the structures first and then hoping humanity will change with it. Sometimes this works, but typically another structure like the previous one pops up in its place.

True changes start within the people themselves. When people change through awareness, structures and organizations change to meet them where they are. The modern world is set into place as it is and the only way for it to become more compassionate and peaceful is for people to realize who they truly are and believe in their power to create the life they desire. When each of us focuses on self-love and living our best life, we begin to collectively change the world to reflect who we are. This is the ultimate goal of each of us choosing to perceive life through a higher conscious perspective.

The path to higher consciousness is choosing to transcend the ego and exist in a higher conscious state of awareness that connects us to the wisdom of Source.

Chapter 2

Ego

As we have started to discuss and explore, we all have egos. Ego is the part of our mind stemming from the illusion of being separated from Source. Ego causes the judging and questioning of everything—it is the thoughts we use to define the status of our education, our cultural expectations, our professional titles, fears, insecurities and has a mental influence on how we think, the beliefs we hold, and how we judge ourselves and others. When asked to describe ourselves in this lifetime, it is mostly the ego aspect of ourselves we will use to paint a picture of who we are. For example, if I described myself as a result of my education, my career title, my marriage status and how I view certain things in life, I would likely be describing my ego self. On the other hand, if I were to say I was an aspect of Source having a human experience, I would be describing my true spiritual self. We are human, so I describe myself to others through my ego qualities and my personality, but I know in my own heart who I truly am, which is an aspect of Source (Soul).

It is important to point out that ego is not the same as our personality, yet they do blend together. Ego consists of thinking and analyzing, while personality is our behavior and mannerisms; personality is joy or the Soul enjoying the human journey while ego is judging. Our personalities are traits we carry through life despite what we learn or experience. An example of my personality is to be fun-loving, talkative, a nature lover and a researcher. These traits have stayed with me throughout much of my life, while my ego beliefs and ideas have changed with my experiences and growth as a person. Neither our ego nor our personality are an aspect of Source, but our personality is the filter through which the human experience happens and thus is what allows us to connect to Source. I have a loving personality that allows me to align with Source, and I am a researcher, which leads me to want to connect to and ask Source for guidance and answers. As a result, I present a lot of questions to Source that many others would not think about or care to ask.

Ego can influence a person's personality because a person may be told to act in a way that is not part of their personality. For example, I was told growing up to be quiet and not to ask so many questions, but I have a talkative and inquisitive personality. As a result, I had to learn to be quiet and to ask fewer questions, so I could fit in with the ego expectations others placed upon me. Source does not think via ego, nor does it have a human personality. Instead it has traits. These traits transcend ego because they include knowing our connection to all things and understanding our true eternal loving nature, and they transcend personality because in the non-physical realm we are unified with Source and do not experience human behaviors and mannerisms. A good way to think of the traits we have in non-physical terms is to think of them as being vibrational. Our non-physical selves carry a frequency or vibration, and this frequency or vibration does not operate through a judgmental mind.

Most people believe their ego is who they truly are, but in reality, it's a temporary mental facade over their personality and their true spiritual selves. There is much ego present in our world since ego is the reason for conquest, pride, success and the need to fit in with others' expectations. Ego leads us to believe we are separate from everything and everyone else. Yet, when the ego filter dissipates, our awareness becomes clear sighted and we once again see beyond the illusions of this world and understand that all Souls were always connected to and part of Source. The bad guy, the villain, the terrorist, the people we can't imagine being a part of God or Source are indeed part of Source having an experience. Yet it's their Soul that is part of Source, not the ego that they have created in this life. It was their ego that led them to cause grievances, not their Soul, so when a person who has an "evil mind" dies, their ego mind dissipates, and the Soul is no longer associated with it. The Soul was always connected to Source, but now it is no longer connecting an ego mind and physical body to the experience.

Ego only influences our perception of this world, it does not dictate to spiritual realms, influence them or alter them. One may believe someone will go to hell after this lifetime, but hell only exists in the ego mind; it is just another illusion created by having a separate mind from Source. If we recognized everyone on a Soul level, we could not help but feel love and compassion for them. Souls always exist in the love and light of Source, so only egos can create the experience of a hellish existence. Some egos do indeed collectively create hellish existences in some places on Earth, but no ego has the power to create the existence of hell outside of the environments humans create.

To have a higher conscious perspective in this lifetime, it helps to understand that we are Souls having an ego or human experience and the perception of this world is a result of our collective ego projections. A higher conscious perspective is a mental state we can exist in that allows us to see truth beyond our irrational ego thinking.

Most believe this world was created by God, but to be clear, the human-ego ways of this world are not created by God. God does not encourage the creation of atrocities, persecute people, or judge them; however, the ego does engage in these activities, and, in this world, ego has free choice to do so. In this sense, the human ego perception is outside the realm of Source and is only a result of furthering our ego thoughts and projections. Consequently, human ego perceptions and actions persist as they are passed from one generation to the next, keeping societies immersed in ego beliefs and illusions. In some cultures, a greater awareness leads newer generations to question and see beyond the short-sighted ego ideas of a culture, but this expansion typically happens in cultural melting pots, not in areas of the world that condemn outside influences. Diversity of lifestyles and cultures can lead to growth beyond the limitations of ego perceptions. Perhaps this is why those who are so lost in their own ego thinking fear diversity so much.

When humans attack one another, it is coming from ego unless it is for defensive survival purposes. Humans, along with the animal kingdom, have a strong instinct to survive, yet this is separate from ego. I have come across many teachings that view the ego as the mind of survival, and for a long while I believed it to be true as well. I thought it was easy to see how ego naturally exists in its more primal state through observation of the animal kingdom. But, by receiving insight from the higher consciousness of Source, I have learned that animals do not have egos, but they do have personalities, and they are living through survival instincts. The human mind likes to give animals and nature personalities that relate to our own human ego actions and ideas, but animals do not have egos, nor do they recognize their own personalities. They do have some awareness of the energy in themselves and others, but this is not an aspect of ego. Instead, our pets have the ability to love unconditionally, and loving unconditionally is part of higher consciousness. Perhaps this is the reason we love them so much and want to be with them. As for wild animals in nature, they can appear to be in constant conflict, even devouring one another, but this, too, is a result of survival, not ego.

Wild animals in nature have an innate drive to survive. Have you ever watched how birds fight and kill? They are beautiful to behold, yet they commit daily what we would consider atrocities in the world of humans. They can be fierce with one another, territorial and predatory, yet it is all survival instinct. The human experience is not immune to committing atrocities, but the difference is that most of our atrocities are committed for reasons of power, revenge, control and influence. Many times, these are cloaked falsely in the need for survival or even the belief that it's the will of God!

So, is ego a necessary tool to help us navigate this world? The answer depends on what world you want to live in and experience. Ego does not help with connecting to the higher consciousness of Source, yet it serves us well in participating in the modern world. As things stand today, if someone wishes to enter the competitive corporate world or wants to participate in sports, the ego will likely serve them in the games of winning and success. In this sense, we could think of the ego mind as a mask we put on to play the competitive games of life. But, after wearing this mask for a while, we may forget who we are underneath and become lost in the character we have created. This is why ego does not help to connect to the higher consciousness of Source—ego keeps us focused on the games of life and uncertain of our spiritual reality.

Unfortunately, when a person loses touch with their true identity, they may feel at times that they just don't know who they truly are, and they may feel they aren't living the life they are supposed to be living. They may also believe this physical life is all that exists, and because of this they will fear their future and even death.

Ego is what we <u>perceive</u> in this lifetime, it influences our personalities, our beliefs and our perceptions. Soul is who we truly <u>are</u>, it is our true self in this lifetime and we can learn to look inside ourselves and connect with our true self at any time. By doing so, we can feel the loving, secure and divine connection to our Source, all while having fun experiencing the personalities we have in this lifetime. There is a beautiful balance in knowing who we truly are (Soul) and enjoying who we are experiencing (personality). Understanding our true nature keeps us from getting lost in the ego illusion of being upset with the world and brings us back to existing in a peaceful state of mind (a higher conscious state of mind). We realize we cannot change how others perceive the world, but we can change how we perceive the world and choose a path of enjoying this human experience.

From a higher conscious perspective, we can have compassion for the people who have lost their way in ego, because they have become mentally disconnected from Source and resistant to receiving the love, security, wellbeing and abundance that is always available to them. Have compassion, yes, but no one needs to tolerate or accept negative, annoying and combative ego actions from another person. Ego issues are not the responsibility of others to fix. We are all on our own journeys of self-discovery and healing, and no one can truly help someone who chooses to get lost in their ego. We cannot force someone to wake up.

Instead, by focusing on healing and helping ourselves, we do our greatest part in helping and healing the human collective. If we put others first (especially those who may be taking advantage of us because their egos are seeking gain and attention), we become weakened, exhausted and distracted from our own needs, which ultimately does nothing to help anyone. A person can be perfectly in alignment with the loving nature of Source and still set boundaries or walk away from a person who cannot control their own ego and disrespects those around them. When someone's ego runs rampant, they are disconnecting themselves from the true, loving nature of Source, and Source is where true love and security lies. So, in this case, it's absolutely OK to love another person's Soul and dislike their ego.

When our conscious awareness transcends our egos, we can see how this world is dualistic and full of contrasts, while also sensing the oneness or connectedness from which we all come. We also begin to recognize the dualistic nature of our own minds, which is the result of the constant tug of war between our higher conscious awareness and our ego thinking.

Regardless of our Soul's purpose for being here, the ego is our personal and collective creation in this lifetime. It is not a spiritual creation, so it does not stay with, or dictate to, our Soul when it pulls away from our physical bodies. Yet if a person has a very strong ego, it can linger energetically in the non-physical, spiritual realm. Ego thought is energy, and some of the energy of the ego mind continues temporarily after death. Depending on how quickly the ego gets out of the way, our physical vibration can affect our non-physical vibration. As a result, we can temporarily create the perception of a non-physical world that resembles human life on Earth. This is why some people who have near death experiences see religious figures and heavenly realms with angels and beings who look human. Because this is their perception of life after death, the ego mind will interpret it as such. An ego belief in nothingness after death may lead a person to perceive nothingness or darkness temporarily, but it's just their ego's interpretation. There is no need to worry about death. Source helps us all return in a loving embrace beyond what we can imagine, and ego mind dissipates with this divine reunion.

As more people become aware of what the ego is and how it affects us, we as a human race will grow tremendously by transcending it. When the ego loses its grip on the human mind, we can collectively align our personalities with the higher consciousness of Source and awaken from this collective ego dream that creates the fearful illusions of this world. During a time of mass human awakening, we can begin to collectively express our true personalities and spiritual traits and live in a higher conscious state of mind.

Conscious thought: It is your thoughts in this moment.
It is what you are thinking right now.

✎Exercise: Understanding the ego and higher conscious mind

When it comes to your conscious thinking, many influences can come into play, but the two predominant influences on your conscious thinking are your ego mind and your higher conscious mind. The mind most of us experience and are influenced by in this world is our ego mind. Your ego mind is your personalized view of this world; it was created by your culture, your upbringing, your education and your experiences of this lifetime. Depending on the area of the world where you grew up or now live, you may have a somewhat predictable ego. In the United States, many egos commonly value material possessions, labels, financial gain, a competitive nature and Judeo-Christian beliefs.

Most men will find pressure to fit into a style and manner that Western society deems masculine, such as being competitive, aloof and a stud with women.

Similarly, women will feel pressure to act and dress in a manner deemed feminine, such as being pretty, supportive and nurturing. Those who go outside of cultural expectations may find resistance from the ego thinking of those around them, but this judgment stems from ego, not from Source.

➤**Part 1:** Write about a time when someone really hurt you emotionally or physically. How do you feel when you think about this person or the event? Write about how this person or event is making you feel.

⌘**Example:** *A friend chose to verbally attack me for no real reason. They betrayed my trust by bringing up things I shared in confidence with them and used those things to humiliate me in front of other people. I felt betrayed, hurt and angry by their actions.*

After you have reflected on this, look at the words you wrote. Are they fearful, angry, or worried? If so, these are your ego thoughts— the thoughts that see the situation based on the beliefs of your current lifetime and ego thinking. Your higher conscious mind knows that nothing can hurt your true self, your spiritual self. Your higher conscious mind knows this world is ultimately an illusion and the dramas created through the free will of competing minds and different ego ideologies is temporary. These dramas develop, unfold and dissipate within your lifetime; they are just part of your journey.

➤**Part 2:** Now think about the same situation you identified in Part 1, but write about it from the perspective of your higher conscious mind (your mind beyond fear, hurt and anger). Try to see the other side of the coin, try to see how the person or event that caused the distress has their own background and beliefs that influence their feelings and actions. Try and think about what happened to them in their own life that led them to be a perpetrator of stress or pain in another person. Realize they, too, are on their own spiritual path and that what you both feel so strongly about in this life is ultimately happening within an illusion (the belief that we are separate from one another). Behind the illusion of this experience is the true awareness of Source having an experience of expansion through us.

Sometimes these personal experiences are so painful that it is difficult to see the other person's reasoning (especially if their ego mind is sick), so please, if this is the case, choose an event happening in the world. This process is for realizing the difference between ego and higher conscious awareness, it is not to upset you. Maybe in the future you can go back and try and see a very painful experience from a higher conscious perspective and even ask for assistance from the higher consciousness of Source to help heal from this experience.

⌘**Example:** *I know my friend who hurt me by betraying me and humiliating me is carrying a lot of pain from their childhood that they have not dealt with. Although I am not the cause of their pain and have nothing to do with it, they carry resentment toward others who did not grow up as they did and thus project this pain onto others by lashing out on them. This does not make their actions acceptable or tolerable; it does, however, explain why they act out by attacking people who are close to them. I have compassion for the pain they carry in their lives, but it is for them to make peace with and not my responsibility.*

Chapter 3

Perception

What Is the World?

When most of us think of the world, we think of continents and oceans existing together on a large sphere floating in outer space in perfect orbit around the sun. We think of the world as home, a place where we are born and die. We think of the world as the global economy, global weather systems, world wars and nations. Some people's view of the world is limited to only their work and family and they see little beyond that. Whatever one's view of the world, it's all a meaningless illusion—meaningless in the sense that we truly do not know what the world is beyond our own perceptions of it. We each have assigned meaning to it, but this does not make it what it is.

The world is an illusion because what we see and feel is nothing more than energy in vibration or molecules of energy creating forms based off of the instructions of a Universe guided by the higher consciousness of Source. We, along with what we see, don't even have a color. What we perceive as color is just a reflection of light, and without light, there is no color to perceive. Molecules, along with the reflection of light, create the illusion of tangible forms that appear quite real to us, but they are not real. Nothing real can die. Only illusions die.

What is real is Source working in conjunction with nature to bring together energies that eventually appear as forms before our eyes. Source does not reside in this world because Source does not live in a world of illusions. Yet Source can experience the illusion through the Soul, which is its connection to this realm of ego and physical life.

The world is not a mistake and the world is not bad. Rather, the world is a magnificent tool to help Source and the Universe expand through the experiences the Soul has here. There is no duality and contrast in the non-physical world of Source. Rather, there is eternal unity and love, so to experience the expansion created through contrasts, Source manifests a world in which duality can seemingly exist.

The World Is What We Perceive It to Be

Nothing in this world means anything except for the meaning we as individuals assign to it. When persuasive individual ideas become generally held by larger groups of people, they become our collectively held views and our reality. Since these perceptions are held by larger numbers of people, it appears they have more value or credence, but they still don't make anything truly what it is.

Our individual views of the world are somewhat dependent upon what geographical location we grew up in, since there will already be a collective perception held by the people who live there. We may choose to follow without question the collectively held views of the culture we are born into, or we may diverge, relying on our own interpretations, depending on our personal interests. Our personal interests may lead us to seek other sources of knowledge or ideologies, which may influence us to perceive the world in a different way than that of those around us.

Each of us may feel we are correct in our personally and collectively held views because they are the views our egos have latched onto as truth, but this does not make our definitions of something the truth of what it is. Actually, it's likely that the majority of us do not know how to see the truth of what anything is in the first place because most of us do not know how to see or think beyond our own five senses.

We experience the world through our senses, but these senses can vary greatly among all living things. Our individually enhanced or limited senses merely create the illusion of the experience we are suited to have while in our physical bodies. There are those who have a stronger sixth sense, and thus may be able to see the energy around bodies and nature, which simply means their experience is to see beyond the normal perception of this reality.

Perhaps this ability to see energy allows them to see a truer reality because it matches what science in our current understanding has also found to be true: our physical reality is made of vibrating energy, or molecules of an element coming together by bonding or sharing electrons. These tiny elements carry different vibrations and attractions, but they are guided by DNA, which is the master programmer. For most people, it's not so fun to think of the world with this bare bones, scientific view, but as of now, it's the best way scientists can describe what is behind the creation of what seems physically real or solid.

I don't think any of us really want to go around thinking of our friends and family as a bunch of molecules coming together to form a being, so it's probably best to see and experience them as we wish to see them. Yet sometimes, reflecting on these types of greater realities can help us bring things into perspective and transcend the trivial ego situations we find ourselves in during this lifetime. For example, when we stop being lost in ego thought and really take a moment to understand that we are made up of energy coming together to create an illusion of solid realness, it can provide the opportunity to form a new belief or transcend the ego beliefs we layer onto this reality.

Once we can see the core of who we are beyond all the mental filters we have created, we have a better chance of putting the pieces of our perceptions back together to form a more positive, healthier and clearer view of the world.

No one's view of the world is incorrect, it is just their chosen view. If it is real to them personally, then it is their truth and the view they are here to have and experience. If a person finds themselves not fitting in with the collectively held views of those around them, they may find comfort in knowing that it's perfectly OK with Source to believe in what makes sense to them. One's chosen belief doesn't affect or change one's eternal connection to Source.

At any given time, one may choose to change their view of life and begin to see the world in a different way, hopefully through a better perception. This choice to perceive differently may have to be limited to one's own mind since there are places in the world that still condemn someone for believing differently, but this condemnation comes from ego, not from God. Even in some free societies of the world, others may find a person's new ideas and perceptions threatening to their own ego's way of life. That is mostly because many of those who choose to get lost in the perceptions of the collective ego do not want something to come along that may make them question their own reality.

A person's new ideas may make others feel uneasy in their own existence, and there is no need to make others uncomfortable by pushing new ideas onto them. If something feels valid to you, yet others are not ready to wrap their heads around it, that's OK. Everyone is on their own journey. Let people exist where they want to mentally exist, as long as where they want to exist is not harmful to anyone.

There are those who become self-righteous in their beliefs by claiming to have the final answer for the truth of creation. This is questionable since ultimately, we all experience our beliefs through our own perceptions and interpretations. If a self-righteous person chooses to put other people's beliefs down, then they are actually out of alignment with Source and do not act upon truth at all. The higher consciousness of Source does not think with a mind under the influence of ego and would not choose to have anyone feel superior and attack another, no matter what they believe. Nor does Source see our true self or Soul as separate from itself. Because the ego mind is separate from higher consciousness, it leads us to believe our Soul is separate from Source, but this is just a small-minded ego projection of our relationship to God.

✍Exercise: What does the world mean to you?

Write about what the world means to you. What did it mean to you when you were younger and what does it mean to you now? How would you like to see the world in the future? There are no right or wrong answers here, just perceptions and reflections. All perceptions are valid since this world is assigned meaning based on how we perceive it. The purpose of this exercise is to encourage you to truly think about what the world is because most of us really do not think about it.

Spiritual Beliefs Become Our Personal Reality

On some level, a person's belief and perceptions of spirituality will be what they in turn experience because people experience what it is they focus their attention on. When someone has an experience that conforms to their beliefs, they will feel a sense of validation in that belief, but by no means does this make their belief the one true belief for all.

All of this comes down to the fact that there is no exact story told by humans to explain our world, the Universe and God. This is because all of our perceptions differ, and not only do they differ, but they are under the influence of the ego mind, which wants to make God act like humans rather than humans act more like God. To understand anything beyond this world we would have to be completely free and clear of all ego filters, which color any type of spiritual truth.

If there were one true story of creation and spiritual existence given to us from Source, it's likely it would not be understood by most human minds. This is because most of us are trained to see everything as separate, so we put everything into buckets, which makes it difficult to understand the oneness of Source. Also, most of us hear what we want to hear so we simply cannot resist taking what we hear and coloring it with our own ego beliefs and perceptions.

Even if people could comprehend the information coming from our one true Source, people would still perceive the meaning of it differently! Source could tell a room full of people a truth about the world, yet each person would take that truth and fit it into their own reality and thus perceive it in their own unique way. With our human ego minds, we simply cannot wrap our heads around thinking in oneness beyond all our separate ideas and perceptions.

We have the choice to create any view we wish when describing the unseen spiritual world or afterlife, but at the core of most beliefs is the consensus that we are Spirit having a human experience. We can individually define this experience as good, majestic and divine or we may choose to perceive it as sinful, flawed and even evil, but it's important to realize what a person believes to be true will ultimately affect their own personal reality.

For example, a person who believes in an unseen evil will likely create the perception of evil, while another person who does not believe in an unseen evil will not have the same experience because this perception is not part of their own reality. It is important for all to realize that what we as individuals choose to believe becomes very real to us personally in this lifetime because the more we focus on something in this ego realm, the more we bring it into our existence.

If someone believes a negative entity is haunting their house, this is the experience that they have. However, it does not mean that their neighbor next door has the same belief or experience. The neighbor who does not believe in such things does not experience the same type of haunting, yet the experience can feel very real to the person who believes it can happen. A parent with a strong belief in the existence of evil ghosts can certainly influence their children to believe in this same reality, but children can grow up and choose to change their perception of this topic (and any topic, for that matter) and move beyond it.

Evil is not part of the non-physical world of Spirit, but it can become a manifested reality for some people living on Earth. Everything is energy, even thought, so what we choose to perceive and believe, we can bring into energetic existence. The belief in evil is common and can be hard to escape since it is so ingrained in the human collective through, our religious beliefs and what we see in popular media (movies, TV, etc.). Because of this programming, many people indeed believe evil entities exist, and by believing, they give energy or creation to an actual existence of evil.

As a result, evil energies will seemingly exist in the minds and experiences of these believers, but it will not exist for those who do not perceive or believe it. It is very important for people to realize they themselves are manifesting and attracting these energies, they do not come from dark souls, fallen angels or curses set through voodoo dolls.

By understanding the power of beliefs, one can see how people are inadvertently manifesting evil or negativity in their own lives. If they believe other people have the power to curse them, it is actually their belief that others hold this power which allows it to happen. Beliefs and perceptions carry energy and create the reality around us that we ultimately experience.

There are many who believe the things that happen to them in life are a result of the world around them. This view is flawed because the world is the effect of our thinking and actions, not the cause. If we were to collectively change how we think and act, our perception of the world would change as a result.

Others believe their lives are a product of fate, making them predestined to be either blessed or cursed in this lifetime. A person with a fateful view of life may also believe they have to pay a spiritual price for something they did that will haunt them for the rest of their lives, and if they carry this belief, it's likely this belief will haunt them just by their perpetuation of it!

But having these beliefs doesn't make them universal truths, it just makes them the individual's own personal truths and as a result, these people manifest their beliefs into existence. If anyone believes they are cursed, the energy of this vibrational thought will rise to meet them where they are—in this case, cursed.

If one does not hold this concept dear and instead they believe they are blessed in this life, then being blessed becomes part of their reality and their experience, and as a result, they attract more blessed situations into their own lives and the lives of those around them.

Creation is the result of an intention putting energy into vibration. This intention may come from the high vibration of Source, or the lower vibration of human thought. I do not mean lower as less than, rather lower meaning people are not fully awake to a greater reality and thus are capable of creating both low (ego) and high vibrational (higher conscious) aspects of life on Earth.

For example, we may create masterful art and architecture (higher conscious) and at the same time make atomic weapons (ego) with the intent to quickly kill massive numbers of people. Luckily the process of thoughts manifesting is slower for humans than it is for Source, because if it weren't, people would be manifesting all of their negative thinking instantly!

Every physical creation on Earth began with Source having the will to experience itself. The illusion of Source being separate from itself is needed to create the contrasts that allow for experiences. Energy comes together to manifest a form that appears to be physical. This happens on all levels of physical creation, but only humans experience having a conscious ego mind.

I will use myself as an example. Source has the will to create an experience, so David's Soul (inner connection to Source) began manifesting or bringing together non-physical energy to create the physical illusion or experience of David. The creation of David carries higher conscious awareness and the ability to create, but David is also influenced by his ego and has not always known what is best for him. So there have been many times David has created beauty, but there have also been times he has been destructive. This is OK because Source is on a journey to experience this lifetime through David and all is in divine order whether he realizes it or not.

Our own view of the world and creation is up to us individually to think about and experience; it's just part of our journey.

When seeking answers as to how and why the world began, a person may choose to look to scientists, spiritualists, philosophers or something else for this understanding. The scientists will measure their theories based on a hypothesis they can measure, while the philosopher will look at the world based on intellectual reasoning. The spiritualist may rely on psychic questioning to probe Spirit and other non-physical energies through mediumship or channeling, yet it's all relative depending on their own personal perceptions and beliefs—relative meaning that the person receiving divine insight can only communicate what they have the mental capacity for understanding.

For instance, if a person does not understand physics themselves, then they would not be able to understand Source giving an explanation through physics. Also, the higher consciousness of Source will try to communicate concepts by presenting as a personality the communicator can recognize and relate to. This is another way someone will feel validated in certain beliefs.

My recommendation for seekers of knowledge, especially when it comes to spiritual creation, is to go forth and seek what resonates with them and have fun on this journey of understanding. It's OK to be open minded and not to stress about right or wrong answers because we are not being judged for the answers we come up with. If we do find answers that resonate with us, then we can take the knowledge in as part of our personal theory of existence and belief.

If anyone comes across information that has no meaning or makes no sense, even if others claim it to be absolute truth, then they should discard it with all due respect to its steadfast believers. It is beneficial to be open to learning more and expanding our beliefs, it allows us to evolve in this lifetime. Also, by existing in an open-minded state we stand in a stronger position when experiences in life come our way that may challenge us and perhaps test what we currently perceive and believe.

Our truth is a result of our own perception, and we may choose to be philosophical, scientific or spiritual about it. We have free will to pick the discipline we will follow, but I hope we all consider uniting these disciplines within our own perception because together they will help bring us an even greater understanding of ourselves and this Earthly existence.

Life Is What We Make of It

We have all heard that "life is what we make of it" at some point in our lives, haven't we? But what exactly does this mean and how do we make anything happen if we don't know how?

Life is full of contradictions and uncertainties and many of us are not even sure what is best for ourselves in the first place. We perceive through what we learn and what we experience, but what we learn can be flawed and our experiences may not have been the best. As a result, we could have a misconstrued and unfortunate perception of life. But, an unfortunate perception does not make life what it is; the perception is just another experience of life that a person has free will to hold on to or not. There is always an opportunity to create a better perception that leads to a better life.

Most people hold some type of a perception of what God is or isn't because it's hard to escape the idea of God, especially in America, where the word God is even printed on our money. Because of a limited exposure or overexposure to the concept of God combined with our personal experiences, we may resent God, worship God or disbelieve in God altogether. It's likely we all have, at one point in our lives, at least questioned if there really is a God. If so, we also likely pondered whether we are supposed to pray to him, her, it— and should we be afraid of God?

For some, the perception of a judgmental God can make them somewhat neurotic, constantly analyzing their actions as if an invisible, scolding parent were sitting on their shoulders judging everything they do. Half the time these people end up doing what they think might be judged as wrong, leading them to feelings of guilt, shame and insecurity.

Who is ultimately the decider of what is right and wrong? In reality, we are the ones judging what is acceptable and what is not based on our perceptions and beliefs. There isn't a voice or an instant message reminding us, "Hey now, you crossed the spiritual line, buddy!"

The ultimate decider of what is right and wrong is not God. It's the people of a culture who collectively decide what is right and wrong. To enforce their rules, they impose their human perceptions on to a higher power, such as God. Over time the people born into these cultures develop a view of God based on the ruling perceptions of their culture, which they accept as truth. As we have seen over and over throughout history, through a type of nationalism, cultures believing their perception of God is the only true belief feel compelled to force this belief on to others.

In reality, it's a type of dominance and a method of controlling other cultures. Anyone can look to the history of today's dominating religions and see the war machine of colonialism that drove their expansion.

It would make more sense if people could realize that we are judging ourselves based on our cultural teachings and not based on some truth of what God is. Choosing how we see God does not make God who or what it is; it just forms one's own belief and perception. Perhaps the universal answer to the question, "is there a God?" is yes, there is a God (Source), but God does not think through a human mind, which is the main reason for all the differences in perceptions!

Many people are trying to define what God is based on the patriarchal roles a father plays in their culture, but that's a short-sighted perception because God is not a human. My perception of God is grander than the human thoughts of any specific culture or person, because God is much more than we are capable of understanding. We can sense and feel the magnificence of God, but we do not have the advanced language and understanding to verbalize exactly what God is.

We must perceive something before we make it happen. There can't be only one true, set guideline to "make" life happen when we all view life through our own perceptions. The "one idea fits all" concept best suits the one human who originally came up with the idea. I am sure they are thrilled they were able to influence and control so many others! But, this isn't so great for the people who have their own perceptions and experiences and have now been convinced they need to fit into the perception of the person who created the rules.

Also, when someone is lost and doesn't know exactly who they are, they are prime targets for a controlling philosophy to step in and recruit them to see things their way.

Many people don't feel like they are worthwhile because they don't have the material objects, personality or looks that they perceive other people as having. I wish people understood that none of these things guarantee the people who have them a peaceful, happy and fulfilling life. There are many unhappy good-looking people and even more unhappy rich people in this world. Look at how many outwardly successful people hurt themselves or turn to substance abuse, or live lonely lives by separating themselves from others.

Some people look to people in their own personal lives who seemed to have figured it out—they are happy, successful, and life for them appears good. Think about how many times we have said to ourselves (you know you have) or heard someone else say, "If I had their wife/husband or if I had his/her job, life would be great!"

That's just not the case. For instance, let's say a person who is feeling empty and is looking outside themselves for fulfilment had the opportunity to step into the shoes of someone who seemingly has it all. Once they stepped into this person's seemingly perfect life, they would now perceive everything wrong with that life because they would still be judging through their own perceptions of emptiness and feelings of inadequacy.

One could also focus on finding the perfect husband or wife to make them happy, but if they have not learned to perceive a life of wholeness and fulfillment for themselves, they will blame that spouse for their continuing unhappiness.

The only way to make life better and more fulfilling is to perceive it as such. Another person, job, outfit or vacation is not going to change our lives. We alone can choose to change our perceptions.

If we admire someone else's life, we don't need to wish we had their life. Instead we can study their personality and their perception of life. What inspires the person we admire, what did they study, what is their outlook on life and how do they behave in difficult situations or even on a daily basis? If they are famous, have they written a book, or have they done an interview where they talk about their beliefs? Maybe they have a philosophy on life to which they attribute their success; perhaps we could try this philosophy out for ourselves.

If we admire another person's life because they were born into money, we may wish we too could have been an heir or heiress. Yes, they are seemingly blessed with fortune, but being born into fortune brings all kinds of issues and struggles—struggles most of us will never understand. Jealous or resentful people tend not to have compassion for people who grow up with money, but they deserve compassion and understanding just like anyone else. Many people born with money didn't learn how to love because they were given money and materials instead of affection, which then leads to all kinds of emotional issues and an unbalanced life. Wealth does not guarantee a person's happiness or fulfillment; instead wealth is just something taken for granted. If children grow up being given material things because their parents are too busy making money to be affectionate, it can lead to self-worth issues, emotional issues and a manipulative personality.

Getting what they want from their parents can become the method for feeling love, and a pattern of manipulation and emotional instability can occur if these people don't get what they want. It can be devastating if a child grows up and gets cut off because now they aren't just losing the money they took for granted, they are also losing what they understood to be their parents' love.

Children who grow up focused on goals and inspirations, children with parents who give them affection because they don't have extra money to give gifts, have an edge when it comes to being emotionally balanced and secure with themselves. The reason is that direct, real, energetic affection from one's family is ultimately more fulfilling than the material things that offer a temporary high and the illusion of love. Also, material representations of love must become more expensive and more frequent to keep alive the perception of the love associated with the gifts; this empty perception of love is exhausting, both financially and mentally.

Yes, these are extreme examples, and there are many various family dynamics and perceptions we could get into, but ultimately, it's a waste of energy to wish to be someone else. It's difficult to see that what looks easy on the outside can be an emotional struggle on the inside. We all need to be compassionate with all people and to understand that, just because someone's life appears to be easy, it does not make it so. If anyone wants a better life for themselves, they can develop their own perception of what this means. Ultimately no one but ourselves stand in the way.

As we have explored, life is what we make of it. The real question is: are we making our own perception of life or is someone or something else creating our perception of life for us? There are many ideas and beliefs imposed upon us and most of us don't even take the time to question them when they lead us to feel unworthy, limited and even confused in our lives. When we find ourselves looking to other things and people to define us or create our perception of life, then we will perceive life in a way that is not our own and not ultimately helpful for us.

*When we begin taking the time to question our perceptions and
discover what is important in our lives, we can begin to
perceive and experience our lives in a way
that is beneficial to our own wellbeing
and to those around us.*

Chapter 4

Fear

Many of us focus our attention on what we are afraid of, which can have an impact on who we become and how we physically feel. Some people may even become obsessed with their fears, leading to phobias such as not wanting to leave their homes. There are irrational fears and rational fears, but it's the irrational fears that receive the most attention. For example, often irrational fears involve thoughts of not being good enough, not feeling worthy enough, the fear of being judged, the fear of not being accepted, the fear of anyone different and the fear of being attacked. For the most part, these fears are irrational because they are the result of our ego minds dwelling on the possibility of a future event occurring that may or may not happen.

Despite the fact that most of the things people fear never actually happen to them or cause real harm, living in fear can become a big part of their mental state of being. Rational fears differ because they can be helpful in keeping us stay safe. For example, we may not cross a road in front of traffic for fear of being hit; we may leave an area for fear of having to experience a natural disaster. We avoid putting our hands on a hot stove for fear of being burned, and we might avoid someone who has the propensity to hurt us. Rational fears are based either on instinct or from a learned experience, and these fears are typically only acknowledged when they are relevant.

While most rational fears pop up in the moment when we need to take action, irrational fears can become a common scenario in some people's minds even if the feared occurrence has never happened to them or never will happen. These people may conjure up various scenarios of what could happen (attack) and how they will respond (defense). When these fears become overpowering and seemingly out of a person's control, they will not only keep a person up at night, but they can also eventually lead them to feeling physically sick. This is because dwelling on irrational fears causes a person to be in a constant defensive state, which is stressful to the body.

One of the biggest irrational fears people focus on is the fear of people who are different from themselves. Many people will focus their attention on stereotyping others who are different as a threat to their physical body or way of life. This results in people becoming closed off or closed minded and existing in a fearful state of being to avoid having anything to do with the person or people they fear.

If these people could get to know the person they deem to be different, they could perhaps see how their fear is indeed irrational. What appears to make someone different is just a physical expression; behind the physical expression, most people want to enjoy life, pursue happiness, love and be loved.

Unfortunately, people who have not been exposed to and who

have not sought out the companionship of others who live in different family structures, cultural structures and economic structures may exist in a defensive state of mind. When presented with the person or thing they feel threatened by, they may become angered or attack without just cause. Further, when people exist in a defensive state of being, they shut themselves off from Source because they are out of alignment with the loving nature and oneness that everyone's true self or Soul is part of. No matter how much any person is perceived to be different, their Soul is connected to and part of the same Source that all other Souls are part of and connected to. This is the reality, but anyone can choose to mentally close themselves off from realizing it.

When a person persists in a mindset of envisioning some type of an attack, they may begin to experience noticeable effects such as physical and mental anxiety, clenching their jaw, tightening their shoulders and wringing their hands. Over time, if a person continues to be in a persistent defensive state they will experience a continual draining of their body's energy resources, which weakens their body and mind. They will notice these negative shifts in their wellbeing, but it's likely they will not be able to make the connection that the cause is their fearful mindset. Instead it's likely they will attribute not feeling well to something outside of themselves.

Whether one makes the connection or not, existing in a defensive state will lead to energy resources being taken away from the proper functioning of one's digestion, immune system, cardiovascular system and nervous system, not to mention the negative impact it has on mental and emotional wellbeing. In the long run, by continually existing in a fearful state of mind, a person is making themselves physically prone to developing illness and disease and overall to experiencing a lower quality of life. Mentally, they become neurotic because instead of focusing their attention on loving themselves and humanity, they focus their attention on all the perceived threats and ill health they are experiencing. In doing so, they are further disconnecting themselves from the higher consciousness of Source. This is very unfortunate because they miss out on the sense of security along with physical and mental wellbeing that Source provides.

In general, the healthy body knows how to heal and take care of itself without the mind's involvement. Our minds can get in the way of healing because we tend to worry, which causes more stress on the body. Our best chance for healing would be to calm the mind, think optimistically and let the body do the work it is meant to do.

If a person must go to the doctor for an emergency or illness, they can let the doctor do what they can, but it is important to stay in a positive and optimistic state of mind to facilitate healing despite any negative prognosis. One should avoid fearing the worst-case scenario because that fear further drains them of energy that could be used for the proper healing of the body. Not only that, by focusing on the worst-case scenario, a person also helps in manifesting it.

At one time, when I was focusing my studies on biology and psychology, I began to believe there was a genetic predisposition to living in fear. I believed the tendency to fear irrationally was programmed instinctively within our genetics and was passed on in families. For those who had a genetic inclination to entertain fearful thinking, I believed they were naturally predisposed to having physical anxiety. I do still believe being in a constant mindset of fearful thinking can lead to physical anxiety, but I no longer believe that the majority of people experiencing anxiety today are genetically predisposed to it.

In modern culture we are exposed to constant tragic stories from all over the world and we are trained to fear other people who want to attack our way of living. When we begin to obsess over these stories and listen to influential people who use fear to gain followers, we put ourselves in a constant defensive mode because we are focusing our attention on being attacked.

If a person does not learn how to see beyond their irrational fears they may spend their lifetime being on edge or needing anti-anxiety meds to relieve themselves of feeling the physical stress their mind is putting on their own body. This, of course, is not medical advice, but in my own opinion I believe a person experiencing anxiety should start analyzing their thinking to find the cause of the anxiety and perhaps use medication temporarily to get immediate relief. We all can attempt to get to the source of what is causing our anxiety and let it go by no longer allowing it to be the focus of our awareness.

There was a time in my life when I was constantly perceiving attacks and I was experiencing debilitating anxiety as a result. I did not make the connection at the time, so I would drink socially to be around others and I would become the life of the party, but during the day I was back to feeling horrible anxiety and fear.

I thought the anxiety provoked my fearful thinking and I began to think the anxiety was a result of something wrong with my body, so I began taking anti-anxiety meds. I loved this medication because I no longer felt the physical symptoms of anxiety, but if I did not have the medication, the anxiety came back in full force. Eventually, I learned to become aware of my thinking and retrain my mind to let go of fear and irrational threats. It sounds simple, but it was a process of practicing meditation and connecting with Source that helped me do this. Eventually, I was able to quit relying on any type of anti-anxiety medication and instead felt a sense of peace and loving acceptance that I had never before felt.

Not only did I once believe there was a genetic cause to fear and anxiety, I also once believed it was part of one's spiritual experience. I have come across spiritual teachers who taught that our Souls bring fear into our current experience because it stems from past life experiences. This led me to believe that we either had to pay for past life actions or we carried a mental remembrance of a painful past life experience that led us to be fearful in this lifetime. As a result, I believed there was not much anyone could do because this was part of our spiritual existence or path; until our Souls healed, we would continue to be damaged, broken or hurt in our current life.

But, from a higher conscious perspective, none of these teachings make any sense. As I focused on developing a higher conscious perspective myself, I began to see the ego influence in these beliefs. It is the ego that believes we are born with fear as a result of karma or the experience of a past life trauma. In actuality, our Souls do not carry pain, separation or fear into this lifetime because our Soul is never separate from Source. It is an aspect of Source experiencing the illusion of separation and individuality, but ultimately our Soul is always part of Spirit and God.

We are not born into life fearing anything, nor are we genetically predisposed to think fearful thoughts; our Souls do not bring or carry any fear into this lifetime.

I now fully understand that we are not genetically predisposed to think about irrational fears nor is there a spiritual cause; it is only a learned ego belief and part of our mental experience while we are here. Some families are more prone to "teach" and display fearful ego thinking, which may affect a child's perception by leading them to also perceive life through a fearful lens, but we are all susceptible to fearful societal programming. Understanding that irrational fears are not an aspect of our true self or Soul is what is most important since this knowing is what allows us to transcend a life of fearful thinking.

✒Exercise: What is holding you back in life?

Fear is one of the biggest reasons people do not take action in life or follow a path their heart desires. Often, people fear the unknown or going to places they have never been, but the fear of being judged or hurt by others is the most common.

There is a strong precedent set by our friends, family and institutions to be "normal" and fit in without caring about how we truly want to express ourselves. For many people, feeling inadequate, judged or unaccepted leads to feeling unworthy and can be mentally detrimental by creating anxiety and depression. As a result, many people will just act as other people expect them to or do nothing at all. But fitting in with other people's expectations instead of following our own heart's desire can lead us to feeling conflicted, sad and even lonely because we are shutting down and hiding who we truly are or desire to be.

To truly be at peace with ourselves and let go of our fears, we need to realize the ego expectations that are keeping us from being who we want to be. Spiritually speaking, being who and what it is we desire to be is what truly brings us into alignment with Source. This is because being our authentic selves brings joy and fulfilment to our lives, which raises our energy or vibration.

➢**Part 1:** It is important to address the fears that are keeping you from feeling and having what it is you want and then to discover what you need to do to move beyond them. Fears must be addressed and released because fear is what will keep you from manifesting or creating what it is you truly desire. Fear creates emotional blocks that keep you from being open and completely upfront with other people about how you feel; fear also blocks you from receiving more fully the love and abundance coming to you from Source.

If you think you are not doing or feeling something because of laziness and procrastination, look deeper—these are typically excuses. If you want something but are not having it, doing it, or being it, blaming it on being lazy is a copout. Many people just become lazy because they feared taking action at some point in their life.

Let's focus on the fears holding you back from experiencing your life to its fullest by listing any fears that are standing in your way. Think about or write down how you want to feel on a day-to-day basis and the things you want to have and create in your life. What fears get in the way when you think about attaining these desires?

⌘**Example:** *I want to feel happy and at peace in my life, but I realize I worry too much about what others think of me because I fear being judged. The fear of being judged is detrimental to feeling* *at peace with myself and affects my happiness because this fear is keeping me from being myself around others.*

➢**Part 2:** After recognizing the fears you wrote in Part 1 of this exercise, work on releasing these fears. It is only you who choose to hold onto these fears. Take your list from the exercise in Part 1 and ponder the ways these fears are irrational and how ultimately, on a higher conscious level, they are nothing more than an illusion you choose to hold on to. By discovering how fears stem from ego and do not have a spiritual foundation, we can more easily move beyond them. Lastly, write an affirmation that states a more positive way to focus on what provokes your fearful thinking.

⌘**Example:** *I realize I worry too much about what others think of me because I fear being judged. I need to understand or remind myself that I am having an experience in this lifetime that is only judged by human egos, not God. I truly want to follow my heart's desire and be myself. At the end of the day, it's really not important what judgmental people think. People who are judgmental are just trying to fit in themselves and are under the influence of ego. I choose to follow my heart's desire and not the illusions I and others have created through our ego thinking. To assist with letting go of fear, I will focus on being more appreciative and thankful for who I am in this life and be more cognizant of judgmental influences that may be making me feel insecure.*

Your true self is an always safe and loved Soul having an ego experience. The experience you choose to have in this lifetime is only judged by yourself and other people's egos, not by Source.

Programming with Fear

Fear programming often begins at an early age for most of us, so it feels as though it is part of our natural state of being, but it is not. As a child, I feared many things. I remember being terrified when the wind picked up and I could hear thunder in the distance. I also remember being terrified of the washing machine when it went out of balance and I was also scared of offices, school or anything institutional. During my journey I once believed some of these fears were a result of my being genetically prone to being fearful. Later I believed my fears had a spiritual cause. But now I realize these fears were learned. With the ability to see from a higher conscious perspective, I realize these fears likely stemmed from often being teased by my family and friends who put ideas into my head as a child: the washing machine was going to explode, or my kindergarten teacher was a wicked witch going to throw me in a boiling pot.

The fear of thunder as a child could possibly be traced back to my parents telling me thunder in the sky was God being angry, and I will never forget that, on my first day of kindergarten, my brothers tormented me by telling me my teacher was a witch and she was going to eat me. I rode the bus with them on my very first day of school and I was completely terrified the whole way there. Yes, these were just childhood fears that I outgrew but they are good examples, and also a good reason not to tease children! I believe that, through self-reflection, most all of us can determine where our fears are stemming from in this lifetime. When we look back to the causes, we may find today's anxiety is stemming from something in the past that is now irrational to hold on to.

Fearful programming can be hard to escape since so much of it is displayed daily in our news media and television shows. We may feel that these programs are harmless, but we can internalize these messages without being aware it is happening. For example, after watching negative or fearful news stories, we may find ourselves angry or fearful despite the event likely having nothing to do with our own personal lives. When we hear about the terrible events that happen to others, we often fear that we may encounter the same fate in the future. This can cause years of worrying over something that may or may not happen in our lifetime. Even if one of these terrible events does happen in our own life in the future, does spending a large amount of time worrying about it make us feel better or create a different outcome? No, instead we will have wasted a lot of mental energy focusing on these fears with a possible detriment to our quality of life and physical health.

Addicted to the Drama

Anyone who spends hours watching news media outlets can become addicted to the dramatic, antagonistic and fearful stories they offer. Typically, the more horrific or upsetting the event, the more viewers the network gets, resulting in higher ratings and revenue. The result: networks will push the envelope on presenting the most fear and drama, so they will become the highest rated and most successful news outlet in the business.

We have control over this, though. We must choose to turn our own negative ego and fearful programming off and focus on keeping our minds inspired, peaceful, and happy by existing in a state of higher conscious awareness. If humanity could collectively begin to do this, the ratings would go down and the money would run dry for the networks who continue to display these negative, fearful stories. Networks are only showing us what they believe we want to see, so when they realize the ratings have changed, they will gladly change the programming to fit what we are now seeking.

Can fear be used for power and control? Absolutely! It is by far the most powerful tool for controlling how individuals think and respond. It's certainly one of the most useful tools a parent will deploy to get their kid to behave: "Do that again and you will be grounded," or "If you do not behave, Santa won't bring you anything!" But, it isn't just children who are susceptible to being controlled through fear. There are many programs geared toward spreading fear to all generations.

One of the most common types of fearful programming is used by those who seek power and influence over massive numbers of people. Those seeking power tend to create the illusion of fear and attack, offering protection from the attack or danger if given the power they seek. It's especially easy to see this in action during the election season in the United States. Candidates will spend millions of dollars with the intention of stimulating fear and doubt concerning other candidates, worldly events and even hot button social topics. Candidates do this not necessarily because they want people to live in fear, but because they want people to fear not voting for them.

But by doing this, these candidates purposefully or inadvertently make the people they are targeting feel unsafe and under attack, and unfortunately these damaging feelings will linger on long after the elections are over. Many of the people who are seeking power create fear inadvertently because they are far removed from the everyday person and not aware of the effects their campaigns have on them. But, when candidates rely on creative political think tanks to help them connect to voters, these think tanks know how to rake through the fears of their base to get a reaction leading people to vote.

The think tanks know which hot button social issues are effective in riling up people's emotions and they will exaggerate them until a person sees these issues as a threat to their own existence, which unfortunately can have a lasting effect on how they think. Campaigns will continue to use these tactics for as long as they continue to be successful in getting candidates elected. It is up to us to realize the damage they do and be offended by them rather than supporting these fear-based tactics. We each can begin to vote for candidates who do not rely on fear-based campaigns and who instead provide positive solutions to our country's needs. It would be helpful to see the candidates for who they are and not judge them as good or bad and right or wrong based solely on their chosen political party. When we vote solely based on what team a person is on, we allow for dysfunctional people who do not have the people's best interest to be elected into leadership roles just because they are on the right team.

Irrational fears can stem from many different sources and experiences in our lives and many of us will not realize how damaging they can be to our reality. If we persistently exist in a fearful mental state, we become exhausted and easily influenced by others, which makes it even harder to decipher what is true and untrue or rational and irrational.

Fortunately, through a greater awareness we can learn to recognize and overcome the mental programming behind our persistent fears and exist in a higher conscious state of mind. In doing so we regain a better sense of reality and are able to see above and beyond the ego-driven fear tactics presented to us daily. To help with this, it's important to first find balance in one's own life by taking time to relax the mind. It is by finding peace of mind that we can become clear minded and level headed, grounded and centered, which will make it easier to see the ego games and motives behind fearful programming.

There are many ways to get grounded and centered (into a higher conscious state of mind) and it is up to us individually to find what helps to get us there. It's common for people to do this through meditating, doing yoga, being creative or being out in nature, but we are all different in our tastes and needs. There is no one way.

It is important, however, that the activity incorporates quiet moments, so a person can allow for their own greater awareness to become present. During these quiet moments, we can also take a moment to check in with how we are feeling emotionally. If we are feeling stressed, it's time for us to find and understand the true cause of the stress. One should not be surprised if they can sometimes trace the source of the stress back to a simple, fearful conversation or news clip that happened during their day. It could be a conversation overheard at the coffee counter at work in which someone was rehashing a story they saw on the news.

When the source of fear programming is located, we can release these thoughts by reminding ourselves how these fears stem from ego thinking and are not necessarily part of our own true reality. Fear is simply a part of the collective human ego experience and ultimately has nothing to do with our true spiritual nature. We do not have to ignore what is going on around us and in the world, but we can free our minds from believing everything that happens is an attack on our own lives. When our own minds are free of this thinking we can have compassion for others who are lost in their ego and fearful thinking, and if given the opportunity, perhaps we can assist them as well in transcending their thinking to find a peaceful state of awareness.

✎Exercise: What are you allowing to program you?

You see the world through your own eyes, so the world appears to you as you choose to see it. It's likely you do not even realize you have a choice as to how you want to see the world, but the world is ultimately a mirror of your own perceptions. For instance, a stranger standing next to you may have a completely different view of the world, so what you both witness in the same moment could be interpreted in entirely different ways. This does not make their interpretation wrong, it just means they have been programed with different beliefs and ways of viewing the world than you.

➤**Part 1:** Make a list of the things that are currently programming you.

⌘**For example:** *the news, Facebook, emails, commercials, magazine articles, a lecturing family member or friend, etc. Next to the items on the list, write whether they are negative or positive depending on how they make you feel.*

➤**Part 2:** Give up the negative programming from your list for at least a week and if you can, give it up longer. For example, turn off the news or stop following negative posts on Facebook if they are a culprit of negativity. You will notice how your world doesn't fall apart. If you take a break for a week or two and go back to watching or reading them, it's very likely the same rehashed stories or quality of stories will still be droning on. You may have missed an important story or two but you benefited greatly by freeing your mind from negative programming.

Because you may have created a habit of looking at many of the things that can be deemed negative, you may need to find something uplifting to do in their place. This is a distraction from the negative habit that can help alleviate the desire to participate in the activity. If it's too hard to turn away from the habit cold turkey, you can make small, incremental steps to change your patterns. Perhaps take one day off from looking at negative programming and then try for longer.

➢**Part 3:** Try to focus more on the positive things you wrote on your list and find some more uplifting things to follow. If it's difficult to give up the daily news stories, check out the website "Good News Network." There are so many positive things happening in this world, and yes, some news actually focuses on these positive events.

Chapter 5

Mind, Body & Soul

The Various Aspects of Mind

I'm sure many of us have thought at times, "My mind is my own worst enemy," or "I don't know why I do the things I do," or "I need to stop analyzing it!" When the mind is left unchecked, it can become a seemingly unstoppable force. The good news? Incessant thoughts are not truly who we are, they are just thoughts we are allowing into our awareness. Because we are not taught methods of removing ourselves from our thoughts, they can seem to dominate or even control our lives. But we can turn our awareness off from these thoughts. Yes, we can indeed have a peaceful mental existence without non-stop thoughts making us feel like we are going crazy.

Not only can we train our minds to be more peaceful and master how we experience this life, we can also build a healthy relationship or connection to the unseen energy that is all around us. Unseen energy is indeed all around us, and we can improve our relationship to both the seen and unseen by improving the quality of our thinking.

If unseen energy sounds strange, then we should ask ourselves, "Can we see our thoughts?" No, we can't, but when we focus on thoughts we give them energy that can lead to the creation of events, emotions and physical feelings. Further, our thoughts are creating the life and environment we exist in, so if we do not bring mindful awareness to our thoughts and our actions, we allow ourselves to live at the whim of someone or something else. We lose all control of the one thing we do have control over—our own thoughts.

I have learned so many terms over the years to describe the mind, but it can be kept simple because it really does not need to be overly complicated. In our human existence, we have our conscious mind, and our subconscious mind. Both minds are important to focus on when trying to get into our own higher conscious state of mind that allows us to connect to the higher consciousness of Source. Our conscious mind exists in the now moment, it guides our attention, so it is here that we decide what we want to mentally focus on or just experience mindful awareness. The conscious mind is also where we do our analytical thinking and entertain our ego thoughts, or it can be where we consciously decide to focus on connecting with Source by quieting our ego thoughts. It is not difficult to recognize our conscious mind since it's the mind we are using to analyze and discuss, but it can be much harder to recognize our subconscious or "automatic mind."

The subconscious mind runs behind the scenes, allowing our conscious thinking to focus on whatever subject we are mentally pursuing at the moment. There is a reciprocal relationship between the conscious and the subconscious mind because whatever we are consciously pursuing or focusing our attention on will program our subconscious mind. The subconscious in turn carries out automatic reactions or qualities of thought and energy that can have an influence on our conscious mind.

It's important to understand this relationship because the quality of our conscious thinking sets the stage for the quality of our subconscious mind. As a result, we may subconsciously feel certain emotions even when we are not consciously thinking about something that correlates to those feelings. For example, someone who entertains a lot of fearful or angry thoughts may be frustrated when they go to do something that they should find fun, but they can't enjoy themselves because they feel an underlying anxiety and tension. They may at first think something is wrong with them or they are not feeling well, but the problem is very likely their negatively programmed subconscious mind, which has been programmed from their past negative conscious thoughts and is now running a theme of fear or anger behind the scenes.

Because the automatic subconscious mind is presenting an underlying sense of unease, it influences the conscious awareness, making the person feel uneasy when currently there is not an outside event to make them feel uneasy. This can be confusing and frustrating for someone who has been stressed for a while and is now trying to have a fun moment but cannot allow the joyful experience of the moment.

Because so much of our thinking is automatic, coming from the subconscious, it is very important to understand that the subconscious is an "effect" or a mental storehouse of the conscious thoughts we are entertaining daily. Beyond the automatic thought responses that we can recognize, the subconscious is also the mind that influences or guides our autonomic bodily processes such as heart rate, breathing, digestion and our flight, fight or freeze response. A fearfully programmed subconscious can keep our body in a perpetually defensive state, which drains our body's resources.

This means a negative or fearfully programmed subconscious can lead to symptoms such as anxiety, rapid heart rate, high blood pressure, shakiness, shallow breathing and even chronic upset stomach or indigestion.

The subconscious also communicates to the non-physical world around us. It may take an act of faith to believe in this connection since most of us cannot detect it, but we do in fact communicate constantly to our spiritual Source though the subconscious. The subconscious is the entry way for divine inspiration and spiritual healing, which occurs when we are in positive alignment with Source. We do not hear voices or see things, but we subconsciously receive this calming, loving sense of wellbeing along with inspiration and healing—all behind the scenes of our conscious awareness. People may interpret this energy in different ways but it all comes from the energy of Source and is translated by us in our unique ways. The thoughts of the subconscious carry a vibration that is always communicating energetically (vibrationally) to Source, explaining what we feel and what we want to manifest in our lives.

All of us receive life force energy from Source, but we close ourselves off from mentally connecting with Source if we have unintentionally programed our subconscious to carry negative vibrational thoughts. To align ourselves with the higher consciousness of Source we need to consciously think positive vibrational thoughts. This act programs our subconscious to align with Source. Emotional blocks happen when we allow negative emotions and fearful thoughts to permeate our minds, keeping us from receiving beneficial energy from Source, which is what truly keeps us inspired and in a state of wellbeing. The process of receiving energy from Source is automatic and beyond most of our conscious awareness. But when we focus on maintaining a positive vibration we can see the result of this spiritual energetic connection as health and as things we desire manifesting in our lives. Source senses and responds to the vibration of our thoughts and feelings, and since the subconscious is the transmitter and receiver, a person will want to be in charge of what conscious thoughts they entertain. Simply put, negativity is out of alignment with Source because negativity is an aspect of ego and ego does not exist in spiritual realms.

It is true that the subconscious has a lot of behind-the-scenes influence over our lives, but it is not beyond our control. Actually, we have the ability to greatly influence it through the quality of thoughts we choose to consciously entertain. Since the subconscious is the mental storehouse of our conscious thoughts, in time we can reprogram the quality of thought energy stored within it by consciously focusing on more positive and beneficial thoughts. For instance, if we recognize that we are having fearful or anxious automatic reactions to normal everyday events, we can begin to consciously focus our awareness on thoughts of optimism, courage, peace and love. In time, we will reprogram the subconscious to carry these thoughts and feelings, which will lead us to have automatic reactions of confidence, happiness, loving kindness and perhaps even humor. Further, positively reprogramming the subconscious mind can lead to a calm demeanor, a relaxed body posture and a calmer nervous system.

When focusing our conscious attention on reprogramming our subconscious mind for health and positivity, it is also important to be aware of outside programming that influences us to think negative thoughts and feel negative emotions. This may require that we avoid certain negative people, especially media commentators whose paid purpose is to upset or shock people. We may also need to avoid television shows and movies based on horror, or music that contains negative lyrics. All of these can have a negative effect on our subconscious mind.

We can watch or read the news to stay informed but it's important to find news that just reports the facts and doesn't offer an opinion on the news. Negative opinions can be quite persuasive, but they are coming from an individual's perception; they are not necessarily truth for all. It's much healthier for us to form our own opinions based on what we consider to be the most important and compelling evidence and not on the biased opinions of others.

Overall, it's very important to understand that anyone we decide to listen to, especially on a daily basis, will have an impact on our thinking, not only in the moment but in the long term. Outside influences can program one's automatic subconscious thinking to act and respond in certain inauthentic ways. One may not consciously agree with a person's judgmental, condescending, hateful, fearful or prejudice speech, but if someone spends their time listening to it then it's likely to influence their own subconscious mind.

Anyone who wants to check in with their subconscious programming can begin by taking note of what they are generally thinking about day in and day out. Are they thinking thoughts of pessimism, fear, hate and anger, or are they having thoughts of optimism, security, love and joy? These thoughts will be a great indicator of what their subconscious is being programmed with and holding onto.

Another way to find this out would be for a person to pay attention to their automatic responses to things that happen to them daily. Do these people automatically respond by getting upset, or do they respond in a calm and patient manner? These emotional responses are also indicators of how the subconscious has been programmed. If anyone determines that they have a negatively programmed subconscious, they can make a conscious effort to begin reprogramming it to be more positive, so they can live a healthier, happier and more peaceful life.

⤷Exercise: Using affirmations to retrain your subconscious

If you have continuously entertained fearful thoughts over a period of time, unfortunately they are now also programmed into your subconscious mind. The subconscious mind is a mental storehouse of your thoughts and feelings and also where most of your automatic responses to daily events come from. Fearful subconscious programming can lead to automatic responses to non-stressful events, such as a racing heart or turning stomach. Don't worry, you can retrain your subconscious mind to be less affected by, or even completely free from these fearful automatic responses.

Meditation can help tremendously in this process, but for now let's focus on affirmations. Affirmations really do work, they are not silly or pointless. When you focus on positive affirmations over and over, they help to reprogram your subconscious mind to be in a positive state of being. Positively reprogramming your subconscious will lead to positive automatic responses and better health for your body.

➢**Part 1:** First, find affirmations that resonate with you. Coming up with your own positive affirmations (such as "I am happy and at peace") is wonderful, but if you need help, you can find hundreds if not thousands of affirmation examples on line. Just search "list of positive affirmations" to find some that resonate with you. Print or write them out, put them around your home, your office, school or in your car and focus your attention on them consistently throughout your day.

Going forward, if something upsets you, focus your attention on the affirmation and not on the upsetting event. Don't allow your mind to focus on or analyze irrational fears. Turn your attention to the positive affirmation instead. By doing this you are mentally canceling out the fear and instead programming your mind with positive and beneficial thoughts. In the future, certain events that would automatically set you off (for example, make your heart race) will no longer have such an effect. Instead you will respond peacefully and calmly to events that irrationally elicit a fearful physical response.

➤**Part 2:** For one week, set a timer (perhaps on your phone) to check in with yourself. You can set any schedule you want: perhaps every hour during the day or maybe three times a day. When the timer goes off, check in on the status or quality of your thoughts. Are you worrying, dreading something, complaining about something, judging yourself or someone else? If so, catch the train of thought while it's happening and focus instead on one of your chosen affirmations—perhaps one that specifically counters the negative thought. By doing this and keeping up with it, you can absolutely retrain your subconscious thinking to be in a more positive and less fearful state. This will also benefit your health because when you eliminate fearful thinking from your subconscious mind, it reduces physical anxiety and the stress put upon your autonomic physical processes.

The Collective Conscious

Beyond our own individual thinking there is a collective conscious that is created by groups of people coming together and making mental agreements about something. These mental agreements create and carry an ego energy that can take on a life of its own. If many people mentally focus on these agreements, the energy around them grows stronger.

For example, collective mental energies bring into existence religious ideas and political ideologies. These collectively held views become so strong they take on an energetic influence that permeates all aspects of certain cultures and geographic regions.

On an even larger scale, the overall collective of humanity assists in creating the experience of dualism here on Earth, such as the belief in good versus evil, or what is right and wrong. All thoughts are energies, so when groups of people focus on ideas or concepts, they "bring to life" these creative ego ideas, which can become quite powerful influences for humans. These powerful collective thoughts will dictate the entirety of many people's lives by influencing and possibly even controlling how they think and feel. Since most people take the collective beliefs of the culture they are born into as truth, they may never see beyond them in this lifetime.

Many collective beliefs are beneficial to people because they provide an understanding of their reality, but some collective beliefs are not beneficial to one's own mind. Concepts that are questionable—such as the idea of negative, unseen forces acting upon our world—can become quite real for the person who believes in them. Concepts of evil, such as demons, poltergeists or even negative aliens, are examples of collective beliefs that are not beneficial to anyone. But for those who believe in them, these concepts do seem quite real. On the other hand, for those who do not believe in these concepts, they simply will not exist in their reality. These concepts are a result of collective beliefs giving power to or creating mental energies, but one must believe in them to perceive them.

When someone taps into the energy of negative collective beliefs and they themselves are not grounded in their own reality, this person becomes a home for this collective energy to latch on to. If this makes some feel uneasy then they can choose not to believe in these collective beliefs and not focus their attention on them. For those who stay in a positive mental space and do not choose to believe or focus attention on negative collective beliefs, the evil simply does not exist in their own reality. At the end of the day, the evil is a human mental creation, there are no evil Souls or evil spiritual existences controlling what we think and believe.

With the modern ability to instantly broadcast information, much of the human collective conscious is attuned to general events happening in our world. These broadcasted events have the power to persuade individual people to think and act in certain ways that are in accord with the collective conscious of large groups of people. For example, in the United States, dueling political influences fight to control the collective conscious programming of a large number of Americans to lead them to lean toward one party or another. Some are consciously aware (knowing) of this programming influence, while others are completely unconscious (unaware) of what is leading them to think, feel and behave in a certain manner. It is by becoming consciously aware of these actions that people are able to wake up to certain programming that has a purposeful intention of influencing their thoughts and actions.

It can be frustrating for an awakened person to be around people who are asleep to the influence of programming because these people tend to not think for themselves. Since these people who are "asleep" think and feel according to the will of collective programming, they think less rationally about why they become upset and obsessed over daily hot button topics. For the awakened person, this not only becomes tiresome, but makes it harder to be around easily programmed people who seem to exist in a state of perpetual upset.

Being in an awakened state of mind brings with it a sensitivity to the energy of those around them; it is very noticeable when people are not consciously feeling for themselves and are instead acting how they are told to feel. When people fit a predetermined mold of thinking, they become quite generic and predictable, which is ultimately the aim of the programming.

When collective programming becomes very negative and combative, people who are awakened and more sensitive may seek a more peaceful existence by surrounding themselves with animals, nature and other like-minded individuals. This is because the awakened person finds it disturbing to be around the vapid thoughts of others who obsess over the negative stories they are told rather than creating their own beautiful life story. Most awakened people have found a way to exist in a higher vibrational conscious state of mind. To remain in this state, they tend to avoid the lower vibration of negative stories being told along with the unaware people who perpetuate them.

As a person mentally evolves, they become even more sensitive because they are in tune with not only their own conscious mind but also the collective of human conscious thoughts. When generally held collective ideas diverge from rational thinking to focus on irrational fears such as the whole world being volatile, the person who is awakened and sensitive will be quick to notice. Yet, those who are asleep will not realize they are being pushed into thinking irratio-nally, and because it's what they are told, they believe it to be true. If more people existed in a higher conscious, awakened state, the world would be a better place. People would rely more on their own intuition instead of what the ego-based, power-seeking propaganda machines are telling them to think. In addition, they also would feel how important it is to be compassionate and at peace with them-selves and those around them.

We all have the ability to create our own life story, and collec-tively we all have the ability to create a better world. Unfortunate-ly, until people wake up or the storytellers decide to weave a more beautiful and optimistic story, this world—for many—will have the illusion of being a scary and tumultuous place.

Soul Manifests the Physical Body

My goal in discussing the Soul is to bring forth an idea of the mechanics of the Soul. It is not an attempt to change what you currently believe. Instead, hopefully this discussion will help to strengthen your beliefs. I have learned much about the Soul through my connection to Source, which I experience as a result of allowing myself to see beyond my ego mind. It took a lot of time and self-work to clarify my mind and some days I too get lost in ego dramas. But when I focus my attention on quieting my ego thoughts and connecting to the higher consciousness of Source, the insights begin to come clearly into my awareness.

The following concepts and beliefs come from my connection to Source and form the basis of this book. If these beliefs resonate with you, incorporate them into your own beliefs. If they do not resonate with you, that is OK too; perhaps this discussion can simply be just another interesting perspective to reflect upon when you are thinking about the Soul.

With a better understanding of how we experience life through the flexibility of our perceptions, it becomes easier for us to recognize that there is more to ourselves than what we see with our own eyes. While it is easy for us to perceive our physical bodies, it is harder to see the non-physical energy body that exists in and all around our physical selves.

Our energy body is a field of energy that connects us to everyone and everything. Everything on our planet, animate or inanimate, has an unseen energy behind its creation and its existence. Some of these creations have a conscious intention we can observe, while others move much slowly and thus seem unconscious (plants, for example). Other creations seem barely to carry a vibration (stones, for example), because it may take centuries for them to be created or even dissolve back into elements; even mountains eventually return to dust.

We tend to think of ourselves as having a Soul that comes as a spark of internal light or an energy that surrounds the body, but this does not appear to be the case. Instead, our Soul attracts or manifests physical energy around its non-physical self to create the appearance of being physical. Our Soul does not really come from someplace else; it is already here, just on another unseen vibration or realm. When our Soul chooses to experience this realm in a physical form, it begins to use energy to manifest a physical body by bringing elements together.

A Soul connection between physical life and Source begins in the mother's womb. It is dependent on the mother's energy as to whether the Soul can continue to manifest a body. If conditions are right, the Soul begins to attract more energy around itself, which leads it to grow in physical size.

There is no perfection in this process since being physical is not being perfect. There are many environmental and emotional influences in this realm that may lead to the creation of a disabled or unhealthy physical body and the Soul will choose to continue on with this creation or not. There are also spiritual reasons why the Soul comes into a body some might label as disabled or sickly, but this is a journey the Soul chooses to experience. Some Souls may choose only to experience a body being created in the womb.

Since the Soul creates the body, the Soul is present throughout the process of a body forming in pregnancy. The Soul does not come "in" to a body during the time of birth; the connection is already there. When the Soul disconnects from its physical creation at some point, the physical body will dismantle back into the elements from which it was created.

Our non-physical Spirit is the part of Source that wishes to have an experience, and our Soul is the inner connection we have to Source while in this physical experience. If we were to be able to see Spirit with our eyes it would appear as white light, but it is not light in the sense we physically think of. We think of light as a brightness from the sun or a light bulb that allows us to see with our eyes, but Spirit is way beyond this type of light.

We can each interpret how it looks and feels to be Spirit, and also when it began and where it's going, because our beliefs are unique to our own perceptions. Ultimately, we are here to have this human experience and we do not need to worry about what everything is supposed to be like in non-physical spiritual realms. We came here to experience the beauty of this life, but when life gets too scary and depressing because we have lost too much of our mental connection to higher consciousness, it is important to remember to calm the ego mind and remember who we are: We truly are a Soul that is always safe and loved. We all have the choice to create peace, joy and happiness in our inner mind by seeing through this higher conscious perspective. When we create inner peace for ourselves, it resonates as an outward peace or energy to others, so no one should be surprised when people are drawn to us and always want to be around us.

Health of Our Energy Body

We easily recognize the need to nourish our physical bodies with food and water, but less so do we recognize the need to nourish our energy body. Just as the quality of the food we eat has a direct effect on the functioning of our physical body, the quality of our thoughts and feelings has a direct impact on the health of our energy body. We do not actually make the energy we carry sick, but this energy can carry the vibration of our negative thoughts and feelings, which can lead to physical sickness.

A healthy energy body simply means we carry positive thoughts and feelings about ourselves and others, an optimistic view of the world, and positive ideas about how we visualize and manifest our lives in the energy around us (our vibe).

An unhealthy energy body conveys the opposite; we carry negative thoughts and feelings about ourselves and others and a pessimistic view of the world in the energy around us, dwelling in the thoughts of yesterday rather than actively visualizing and manifesting the life we want.

It can be difficult for some to exist in a state of awareness regarding their energy body since we cannot see it and we are not taught about it through traditional health and science courses. Nonetheless, we do have the ability to recognize and sense it. I think most of us can agree we have felt a negative vibe or positive vibe about someone without the person even needing to speak. It's easiest to notice the energy of another when something is emotionally wrong with them because their unsettled vibe makes others uncomfortable to be in their presence.

This happens when someone is mentally focusing on something negative and they begin to carry the negative vibration of those feelings in their energy body. Another person can feel their negative energy and it's likely they do not want to spend too much of their time in the presence of it.

On the other hand, we can feel an awareness and even an attraction to the positive and healthy glow around someone who has a joyous and optimistic mindset. Positive-thinking people can be very attractive to others, not necessarily because they are physically beautiful, but because they are carrying a beautiful, positive energy around them that is an attractive energy to be around. It feels good to be in the energy or vibe of a person who is projecting a happy and positive energy. Their positive energy can be infectious, and it can make the people around them feel better, too. Also, some people have a very grounded and secure vibe and when people are around them they tend to feel as if everything is OK.

True attraction to another person happens on the energy body level. Yes, we are attracted to someone's personality, but ultimately it feels good to be around a person's positive energy. One should not focus on a person's physical beauty and ignore their energy, for there are many physically beautiful people who are enjoyable to look at but carry a negative energy around themselves. Being attracted to another's physical beauty is an ego attraction and if one chooses to be with someone who is physically beautiful but carries a negative vibe, the relationship is not going to be easy or healthy. The saying "don't judge a book by a cover" exactly fits this concept, meaning: don't fall for looks, fall for what's inside or the energy one carries.

The person carrying a healthy energy body is going to bring forth a beautiful life experience for themselves and for those around them no matter their physical appearance. The person with a negative vibe can develop a void that feeds off of other people's energy, so they will use other people to find their joy and fulfill their needs because they have lost the ability to create and carry positive energy for themselves.

It may be easy to sense or feel the energy of others, especially when it differs from our own, but it may be harder to sense our own energy because we are used to feeling it. Yet one's own energy or vibe is what is most important to their own health. If a person already exists in a positive and optimistic state of being, they do not need to focus on changing how they think. But for those in a negative state of mind, change should be considered.

It can be hard for someone to realize they are existing in a negative mental state because they have become accustomed to feeling their negative thoughts and feelings. Unfortunately, if a person cannot recognize their negative thinking, they likely will not realize how it repels positive people or the effect it may be having on their physical body. Negative or disturbed thinking can create unseen energy blockages in one's energy body, and in time these blockages can manifest into physical issues. Some people may get physical indicators of their negative energy field when they experience unexplained aches and pains or sickness in certain areas of the physical body, but many times these physical disturbances either go unnoticed or a connection to the true cause is not made. Energy blocks, of course, are not the only source for sickness. Positive-thinking people get sick too, but a person with a negative outlook is more prone to illness due to the negative energy blockages they are carrying.

From a holistic perspective, we are mind, body and Soul. So, to be healthy we must focus on the health of our thoughts and our bodies while also understanding our Souls' connection to Source. It is important to realize our bodies include both our physical and energetic body. Awakening to our true spiritual nature allows us to quickly realize when we are under the influence of ego, which wants to put us back to being mentally asleep. With this awareness we can override our ego thoughts and more easily get back to a higher conscious state of being.

When we are in a higher conscious state beyond ego, it's easier for us to focus on positive thoughts and feelings, which then lead us to having a healthy energy body. A healthy energy body, along with nutritional foods, will help bring wellbeing and health to the physical body.

✎Exercise: Finding ways to balance and uplift your energy

Our daily activities can sometimes wear us out and bring our energy down, so it's important for each of us to find balance, physically and mentally. There are many different ways to do this, but I will share some ideas for those who need help getting started. Some of these are common sense ideas, but perhaps they will be a good reminder.

Food: Foods that obtain their energy directly from the sun can be the healthiest choices in maintaining the balance of your physical body. They contain the most life force energy and can also help to balance out any unhealthy or heavy eating. We all can get carried away with eating heavy and decadent foods, especially around the holidays or when we are weary, so be sure to add balancing foods especially during these times.

Exercise: Exercise results in having more energy and releasing stress. It also helps to balance the body by getting your blood moving, your heart working, and detoxing through sweating. If you don't like exercising, find some type of movement that feels good. If you don't like to sweat while exercising, go to a sauna if you can.

Creativity/Art: Creativity can be inspired by our spiritual connection, and when it brings us joy it brings us into alignment with the higher vibration of Source. Art can also be an outlet to express and release inner pain and conflict. Admiring art can take us away from our ego thoughts and worries by inspiring, soothing and calming the mind.

Crystals: Keeping crystals around yourself and your home helps to balance your energy body and your living space. Crystals are proven to hold certain energetic frequencies, so if you are looking for more energy, finding the right crystal is important. It's fun and easy to research the right crystals for you by going to a shop or looking on-line. But, there is no need to overanalyze them because most likely you will be attracted to the right one when you see it.

Essential oils: Essential oils are high vibrational. Diffusing them helps to repel and dissipate lower vibrational energy in the atmosphere you are in. They are medicinal and can help with ailments such as sinus problems, trouble sleeping and trouble relaxing. Finding the ones to use is as easy as searching online. For example, if you are looking for essential oils to help with sinus issues you could simply search the phrase "essential oils for sinuses."

Music: Listening to classical or soothing music is also high vibrational, so it too helps to clear the negative energy in the atmosphere of a space. It also helps to calm the mind and relax the body.

Light: By letting a lot of natural light into your home or work space you help to brighten the mood and kill germs and bacteria. Getting some sun on yourself is uplifting, healing and even helps your body generate essential vitamins. Common sense warning: do not allow yourself to burn!

Plants: Keeping a relationship with plants by gardening or keeping house plants helps to beautify a space, clean the air and even provide a person with a sense of purpose. Plants' flowers and growth inspire creativity and beauty and also a sense of reward for helping them thrive.

Water: Keeping a fountain or living by flowing water helps to bring a soothing effect into your living space. Fountains create serenity and calm and create a higher vibration space. They can also help to bring essential moisture to a home or space that is too dry for healthy skin and breathing. The negative ions the splashing produces helps to clean the air and reduce odors.

Cleaning: Cleaning your home creates healthiness and brings a sense of pride into your space. Cleaning your windows allows more light and brightness to come into your space and uplift you.

Nature: Being in nature is grounding to our energy because we are part of nature ourselves. Observing nature brings peace of mind by allowing us to have mindful moments and bring our awareness into the present moment. The fresh air of nature is healthy to breath and we get physical exercise by walking or hiking its terrain.

➢**Part 1:** What do you do to balance and uplift your energy? Are these strategies working for you? What are some other things you can do to help balance and uplift your energy? Try and incorporate what you find into your life and living space.

➢**Part 2:** Make a commitment to get out into nature at least once a week. If that's not possible, try and create a natural environment in part of your home by getting some house plants, stones and a fountain.

The Effect Thoughts Have on Our Energy Body

We do not need to physically see our energy body to know if it is healthy or not. In fact, there are many parts to ourselves that we are unable to see. Everything that we are—our Soul, mind, energy body, physical body—are not separate compartments. Instead, they all intertwine to make up who and what we are. Some aspects of ourselves we can see, some aspects we can only be aware of, and other aspects of our non-physical selves we will not need to know much about in this lifetime.

In a way, one could think of our physical experience as being like an onion: there are many layers to an onion, but all of these layers together make up the whole onion. When we peel back the papery outer surface of an onion we may come across an unhealthy-looking section of the onion and we may notice how it traverses many layers.

Just like an onion, there are many layers to ourselves, but we do not need to dissect all the layers of who we are to find everything not right with each section. Instead we can focus on the cause of our wellbeing, which is first understanding that we are a Soul connected to our Source, and second, knowing that our life experience is dictated by our mental health or quality of thinking. The purest or healthiest state we could exist in would be a peaceful and happy state of mind, which has a beneficial influence on all aspects or layers of our physical experience. This, along with a healthy diet, will create what we can see and feel as wellbeing in our physical body.

As part of maintaining the health of the energy body, I recommend paying attention daily to the quality of one's thoughts. The process I use for keeping my own energy body clean and clear of negative blockages is to periodically check the quality of my thoughts and feelings. If I feel uneasy or troubled, I take some time to analyze my thoughts and figure out the source of the unease. In doing so I am usually able to discover what's causing the thoughts/ or feelings. It is by becoming consciously aware of the cause that I can work on letting it go. It may be something such as needing to forgive myself or forgive someone else, or it could be that I just need to see something from a higher perspective that allows me to see beyond my limited ego thinking.

It is because we view life situations from a limited ego perspective that we allow ourselves to get caught up in negative thoughts in the first place. If we cannot find the source of an uneasy mental state of mind, we may also need to look at what we have physically done to ourselves. If the body is drained or depleted from lack of rest, not eating well or even partying too much, we begin to feel physically unwell, which in turn influences our mental state of being. Our minds and bodies work together, so when we feel physically depleted we need to find some alone time, rest, drink lots of water and eat some healthy fruits and greens. With rest and nourishment, our bodies become grounded and our minds become clear and centered. When we are grounded and centered, it becomes easier to handle the thoughts and feelings we experience.

Another way to heal or keep the energy body in a high vibrational healthy state is to have a mindful moment or meditate, which I cover in more depth later in this book. Meditation calms and clears one's mind by quieting ego thoughts, and during this time Source is able to help balance and heal the physical and energy bodies. If one cannot quiet their thoughts to meditate, perhaps because they are upset or just having trouble controlling their thoughts, then they can focus on affirmations. There are times in all our lives when something will enrage us, and it is fine to experience that feeling in the moment, but it is crucial we recognize it and then move past it. In the moment of being very upset it's nearly impossible to turn to meditation, so in these situations it is helpful to use positive affirmations to help guide our mental focus. When focusing on positive affirmations, a person moves their focus from low vibrational negative thinking to high vibrational positive thinking. Eventually, by focusing on an affirmation, a person will bring their mind back into a naturally positive and relaxed state of being. While stating affirmations, it is also helpful to take long, deep breaths, which will also help to calm the body.

Personally, when I get upset, I focus on the affirmation, "I am happy and at peace in this moment." I also focus on deep breathing and visualize releasing any negative thoughts on the out breath. By doing so, I am able to get beyond the negative ego moment and back to being in positive higher conscious state of awareness. Yes, the negative thought may resurface later, but I do not give up; again, as needed, I will affirm my positive intention and work to release the negative energy of it.

Conscious intention is the most powerful tool we have to clear our energy body from negativity. Not only can we do this for ourselves, but we can use our intention to help others who are struggling to do it for themselves. This is done by visualizing their well-being and stating positive affirmations on their behalf, but they must be open and receptive to receiving it. One cannot positively (or negatively) have an effect on another through thought alone if the person meant to receive it is not open to it.

As for anyone who struggles with believing in their own mental ability to heal their minds and bodies, there are many tools they can rely on. Tools can also be used for those who know their ability but just need a reminder, or those who are struggling in the current moment to maintain a healthy, positive intention for themselves. Tools do not carry some sort of magic (there are no magic wands). Instead, it is through one's own belief in the positive effect of the tool and not necessarily the tool itself that benefits a person. When a person uses the tool (or has it in their presence), their belief in the tool is what aligns their conscious thinking to a positive state.

When it comes to spirituality and religion, there are many types of relics, emblems and tools used to hold a blessed or spiritual positive intention. Some people may wear a cross or type of crystal, keep a Buddha statue or cross in the house, put a Mezuzah at the front door or use holy water. People may research tools that someone has labeled as having a certain quality and then buy them based on said intention, but a person can assign their own intention to anything.

I like using spiritual tools because they are a great reminder for me to stay in a positive state of mind. I also believe they hold the energy of my positive intention in place so, even when I'm not consciously focusing on positive intentions, the item or tool is still holding the intention for me.

A person can buy a tool from someone who specializes in making them, or they can make or find the tools (crystals/stones) themselves. When creating spiritual tools, a person programs positive intention such as healing or protection into the tool, leading them to carry the positive intention. These objects are still what they naturally are, but they can hold some of the energy a person places upon them.

Some of the tools I like to buy for energy cleansing and protection are crystals, sage, crystal healing bowls and essential oils. Some tools I like to make are crystal elixirs, essential oil sprays and salt scrubs. If anyone is not into making things themselves, there are many environmental sprays involving crystals, sage, cedar, palo santo and other essential oil products made by someone who has perfected their combinations and programmed them with an appropriate intention. There are lots of various tools to use if we are inclined to use them, we just need to research them and use whatever resonates with us.

The energy body does hold many indicators of our mental and physical health, but since we cannot see our energy body, it is important to focus on the cause of its health. Nothing is more healing to our energy body than our positive thoughts and healthy food and water. Yes, tools are fun to have and use but they are not necessary. It is our own good intentions and healthy thoughts that truly guide the energy field of our body. In the next chapters I will discuss how the thoughts and feelings we carry in our energy are more than just influences on health, they are also the blueprint or story we are creating for our lives.

Chapter 6

Creating Our Best Life Through a Higher Conscious State of Mind

Getting ourselves into a higher conscious state of awareness
connects us to the creative and unlimited higher
consciousness of Source.
Through this connection, Source provides us endless
ideas and opportunities to help live
life to the fullest!

Our Own Intuition Is the Most Accurate Guide

We all have our own truths, because our truths are a result of our unique personal experiences and education. It is fine to live by our own truths as long as they bring us peace of mind and we do not force them upon another. When someone tries to tell another person what they believe is the only truth, in reality it is always false. Not only because one's truth is a result of their own individual experience, but more importantly because the individualized experience is an illusion to begin with. Truth cannot be found by looking at the illusion of separateness, it will only be found through a higher conscious perspective that shows us that we are all connected.

The way to see or feel beyond the illusion of separateness is not through our traditional human schooling; instead it is through our own intuition, which comes from our connection to Source. Our connection with Source is strengthened by quieting our ego mind and getting ourselves into a higher conscious state of awareness; it is not found in a book or some other non-physical world.

Source is connected to all that is, and because we have a connection to Source, we can access the wisdom and guidance that exists beyond our ego thinking. To help with this, one could view the ego mind as the mind of illusions and our higher conscious state of mind as the mind of truths. By existing in a higher conscious state of mind we can mentally connect with Source to receive better solutions and higher truths.

The reason many of us disconnect from or disregard our intuition is that we are taught to focus on the issue at hand by relying on our ego thinking. This keeps us more focused on the problem rather than the solution because the best solution is found by seeing above and beyond the problem. Our ego mind likes to rehash our issues and problems by playing them over and over in our minds, which only leads to frustration, thus taking us further out of alignment with our intuitive guidance. It is only by quieting the ego mind that we allow for the higher consciousness of Source to connect to us through our intuition, and when it does, we will have the ah-ha moment of knowing.

In the beginning, when someone is not used to relying on intuition, they may be confused as to whether something was an intuitive thought or a thought coming from ego. Intuition is a gut feeling or a sudden flash of insight, which feels inspiring and even energizing. Ego is more analytical. It runs all the possible outcomes related to the event through the mind, but the outcomes are only the ones we can consciously think of. Intuition can bring to the table something we are not seeing or thinking. It is by recognizing our intuition that it strengthens, and we begin to see it as something separate and beneficial beyond our limited ego thinking. Intuition is guidance that is always in our best interest because it is both protective and loving, while ego thoughts can make us feel as though we are running in circles and creating even bigger problems for ourselves. By becoming heart-centered (compassionate toward humanity and ourselves) and grounded (letting go of fearful thinking and being in the now moment), we expand our intuition, which leads us to further bypass our ego filters. By trusting the loving guidance of intuition, we allow it to further expand into our awareness, which in effect brings forth even more spiritual insight and guiding wisdom. This guidance can show us glimpses of possible future paths and outcomes for our lives and even the lives of others, while at other times it just provides a sense of love and belonging.

There are some who are "gifted" with a naturally strong intuitive guidance (psychics) and are still ruled by ego, but these people are on their own journey in life. I put gifted in quotations because if a person is lost in ego, the gift of being psychic can keep them focused on energies outside of themselves and not focused on progressing spiritually and healing their own lives. It is best to first figure out our own ego issues before moving forward with further developing psychic abilities because the focus on being psychic can take our attention outward while intuition takes us inward. If we are unable to first figure things out and find balance in our own lives, then we will just slap our limited and unbalanced ego views onto higher concepts and they will no longer be higher or true.

A good example of this would be when someone who is fearful and believes evil exists (negative fear-based energies only manifest for those who focus on them) begins working with psychic concepts before sorting out their own mind and reality. If this type of person is entertaining negative types of thoughts and thus holds the belief in evil entities as truth, they will add their beliefs to the unseen energies happening outside themselves. The reality is that what they are sensing is merely a reflection of their own thoughts and inner turmoil. If there were an evil in oneness, which we are ultimately all part of, then we would all experience these evil unseen forces, but we do not. They are limited to those who focus on them as part of their own reality.

As for a psychic who is grounded and at peace in their own life, they can connect with beautiful messages coming from Source. They may apply their own mental filters to these messages and interpret them as coming from an angel, a past religious figure or a being that they may give a name, but names are only needed for our ego minds to better understand the message. Source and the energy (higher consciousness) it uses to communicate to us does not have a name.

Because we as humans interpret things as individual and separate it can be hard for us to understand how a message can come from a collective of higher consciousness that exists in oneness or unity, so we may interpret the message through our own mental filters as coming from a separate non-physical entity. It does not matter if we mentally perceive the message as coming from a non-physical individual; what matters is that we receive the message being given.

By following our own intuition, we become our own best belief and guidance system, and by believing in our intuition, we further believe in ourselves and our own creative power. Intuition helps guide us to be who we wish to be and gives us the courage to go where it is we want to go in this life. Intuition becomes even stronger when we believe in our own magnificence and feel worthy of receiving. The more magnificent we realize we are, the more we realize it is our divine right to know and experience all we wish to experience in this lifetime. It's time we all cast our limited ego perspectives to the side, begin to believe in our own magnificence and trust in our intuition.

The Law of Attraction

The law of attraction is real & universally present in our lives.

Most all of us are familiar with or have at least heard of the law of attraction. It brings to mind the creation of vision boards and lists to tell the Universe what to bring us. It makes one think, "If I just focus on the things I want long enough, the Universe will bring them to me."

Unfortunately, people haven't realized that focusing on wants alone isn't how it works. When the law of attraction was given a lot of media publicity about twenty-five years ago, many people got excited and attempted to put the law into personal use. The concept sounded so easy, requiring such little effort, but how the law is always working and always responding to the vibration of our thoughts and feelings was lost on most.

We don't always think about our thoughts and feelings as being what defines our human experience; instead we like to define ourselves through our titles and belongings. But the Universe is not responding to ego titles or our belongings themselves. The feelings we have regarding the titles and belongings does hold a vibration, which the Universe responds to. But making a list of titles and belongings alone will not work because the Universe is not responding to our verbal or written commands. It is responding to the vibration we carry, the vibration of our overall thoughts and feelings.

Years before my metaphysical studies and real understanding of the workings of the law of attraction, I tried putting the law to use by creating my own vision board. I bought a nice sturdy pin board and got markers, stickers, tape and magazines to cut out pictures of things I liked. I decorated my board with a fabulous home, vacations, beautiful items and I even taped a dollar bill to it. Why not try it out?

Creating it was fun and easy enough. I was excited about my collage of pretty pictures and words, so I placed it on the kitchen counter where I could see it. It sat there with all its fancy pictures for about a week or two. Soon enough, I needed the space for cooking, so I moved the vision board to a table in the mudroom near my back-entry way. In the beginning I would look at it when I came and went and feel optimistic it would work, but as time passed I noticed it less and less. I was usually in a hurry to get out the door, and when I came home I always had two loving dogs all over me.

Eventually, I forgot about the vision board even being there until my friend pointed it out, asking what it was. I then realized it was getting a little dusty and looking a little tacky with some of the pictures curling and losing their luster. I felt silly when my friend laughed about the idea of the Universe bringing me anything and he also laughed about some of the frivolous things I put on it. Later that evening after he left, I put the decorated board in a coat closet and decided if the law of attraction was going to work it will work either on the counter or put away in a closet; it shouldn't make a difference. The concept of how to properly use the law of attraction was clearly lost on me.

Several years later I was packing to move out of my home and I found the vision board in the back of the closet. It was tattered and lackluster with some of the photos falling off. As I looked it over, several of the things I had wanted now seemed silly, and I wondered what I was thinking even wanting them. I took some of the photos off and everything else including the board went into a big black trash bag along with all the other things I was purging from my life. The idea of the law of attraction faded away and I no longer thought much about it. I'm sure there are many other people who had similar experiences as mine by giving the law of attraction a try, but then becoming doubtful and eventually growing bored with the concept.

So what went wrong with the law of attraction working for us? Well, for those of us who do not have a metaphysical understanding to start with, we get a little glimpse into a fascinating metaphysical concept and we hear what we want to hear. In this case, what we hear is, "Get what you want simply by focusing on the item with little physical effort."

We then take what we want to hear and apply it to what we currently believe or think. After we create our personal synopsis of the concept, we find the easiest and quickest route to making it useful in our lives, which for many was making a vision board. The problem is that the law of attraction does not respond to our creative shortcuts such as written lists or pictures. The only person responding to those is the person who created them.

Lists may inspire us and possibly motivate us to stay mentally focused on feeling what we want, but they do not command the Universe to bring it. In fact, telling the Universe what to do by visualizing an object, writing lists or making a collage of pictures is of no use if we're not first in vibrational alignment with the things we want. As my Metaphysical teacher Dr. Paul Masters said, "It's like putting bread into the toaster but not having the toaster plugged in, so you never get the toast!" We can state all the material things we want to the Universe, but if we are not mentally aligning ourselves with the higher consciousness of Source and we are not focusing on what it feels like to have it already, then we are not getting the benefits of using the law of attraction.

Before a person begins working with any metaphysical concept or universal law, they first need to take a look at their own beliefs that could be standing in the way. Some of our programmed beliefs can form mental roadblocks to truly understanding a metaphysical concept such as the law of attraction. If we can't first understand a concept because of our mental filters, we will not be able to put it to use in our lives. As I discussed in the energy body section, we carry around our beliefs, thoughts and feelings in our energy field. This field of energy around us is what does the actual attracting. If a person writes a list of wants but does not carry the vibrational energy of the want in their energy field, they are wasting their time trying to make use of the law of attraction. Also, if they are not existing in a higher vibrational state of being, they are likely creating energetic blocks in their energy field.

There are many things that can lead to blocks in our energy field, and some may actually keep our energy existing in a low vibration.

Let's explore some of these mental roadblocks that interfere with using the law of attraction:

- Thinking our ego knows what is best for us
- Feeling unworthy
- Feeling we must pray to a higher power or God to receive
- Worrying about our past and future

Once we address these blocks that stand in the way of understanding the law of attraction we can move forward in manifesting.

Thinking the Ego Knows What Is Best for Us

The ego wants what it wants, and it wants it now! When first hearing about the law of attraction, we immediately think of how we can use it to get our material ego wants. The challenge is that what our ego wants is not always in alignment with our true best interests. For example, many people think their problems would be solved and they would be happy if they received a financial jackpot, but they couldn't be any more wrong. Statistically, it has been proven that when someone who is not used to having a large amount of money receives a financial windfall, it can actually turn their life upside down. Their problems are not solved by money because they were not mentally grounded in the first place. Instead of providing a sense of true fulfilment, money just brought more issues and other people's agendas into their lives. In a frenzy they spend money to keep up with the goal of feeling fulfilled, and before they know it, the money's all gone.

This does not just happen when receiving large sums of money. There are many who work very hard so they can afford to buy new cars, the latest fashions, the latest phone or larger homes to make them feel fulfilled. But they are not living in the moment or truly enjoying life because they have created a cycle. They spend most of their time working, and when they do have free time they spend it seeking the temporary fulfillment of buying something new. The reason they always need something new is because these things are not what truly fulfills them, they are just bringing them a temporary high of excitement. When the high wears off, they feel a sense of lacking again, which leads them to once again feel the need to buy the next shiny new toy.

This same cycle happens with attraction to other people as well. Many people do not know how to feel fulfilled themselves, so they blame their emptiness on not having found Mr. or Miss perfect to complete them. This leads many people to marathon dating because, until someone can be happy and at peace with themselves, there really is no perfect person to complete them.

Yet, there are those with a personally unfulfilled mindset who will eventually find someone who captivates them with a beautiful body or entertaining personality, and then they will pursue trying to be with them or having them as a possession. This is a big mistake. An unfulfilled person will believe that their happiness depends on the other person, but after a while the infatuation will wear off and they will blame the other person for not meeting their expectations. The person they found did not change; when the infatuation wears off the feeling of not being fulfilled remains, which in reality is no one's fault but their own.

No one can truly make another person happy inside; happiness is only found within one's self. Successful relationships are based on two people who know how to find happiness for themselves and choose to share this joy with another.

What I am trying to get at with these examples is that true fulfilment comes from within. What does "within" mean? It means knowing we are a Soul connected to all that is. It's knowing we are never truly alone, we are never forsaken, we are never judged; instead we are wholly loved and playing a part in a bigger picture.

One of the first blocks to overcome in understanding the law of attraction is knowing that what we truly are and what we truly want comes from feeling good and not from our ego wants. The ego will have us look to the outside world for our fulfillment, but the reality is, the outside world will only temporarily fulfil us. It is feeling good about ourselves and what we want that helps bring more of the good feelings into our existence.

Feeling Unworthy

Fear carries a negative vibration and it's the surest way to take us out of alignment with manifesting what it is we want in life. Perhaps a person fears not having enough money to pay bills. Of course, no one truly wants to live in fear, especially the fear of being homeless or hungry. So, it makes sense that a person wants security and the ability to pay bills. But if they want security yet focus on the fear of not having it, they are creating a vibration around themselves that is resistant to having security.

Even worse, it makes a person feel bad to want something they believe they don't deserve. The feeling of being unworthy carries a negative vibration, thus further putting them out of alignment with receiving what they want through the law of attraction. We are all worthy, we just need to believe it, or even better, know that we are. Unfortunately, so many of us have been led to believe that we are not worthy of much.

Feelings of unworthiness will certainly take a person out of vibrational alignment with achieving success because the law of attraction responds to the positive vibration of feeling successful. It does not respond to feelings of lack and unworthiness. A person feeling those feelings is already creating and experiencing enough of that in their life.

Through an understanding of metaphysics, a person practicing the law of attraction will understand they are always worthy and deserving of everything the Universe has to offer, and they will focus their attention on what is their divine right. The Universe does not listen to our words, nor does it see us as our human body. We are perceived as energy, and the Universe responds to the energy or vibe we are giving off. So, if we feel worthy, then we are, and so it is!

Feeling the Need to Pray to a Higher Power

The song by MC Hammer "You Got to Pray Just to Make It Today" pops into my mind when I think about this topic. It's true, so many of us feel we do not have any power ourselves to create the life we want, or we are victims of a God who decides to bless or curse our lives.

Feeling the need to pray is based on the belief that we are separate from God or Source. Because we feel alone and separate in this world we may also begin to believe we are forsaken or forgotten, which leads some to plead with God for help when things get really tough, scary or lonely. Prayer to God or Source when in desperation does not work to help our situation because it comes from a place of fear (ego), which is out of alignment with the higher vibration of our Source. Prayer can, however, be effective in bringing a person into alignment with God or Source, but only if the prayer is of gratitude, love for God or something else positive (higher conscious).

If the act of praying makes us feel better, then it is beneficial because feeling good creates a more positive vibration. Prayers are thoughts, and thoughts are energy, so prayers carry a vibration as all energy does. Depending on the quality of thought put into the prayer, it will either help to create an energetic alignment with the higher consciousness of Source or create blocks. It does not help to send prayers of desperation and fear, because they are only helping to form more energetic resistance to receiving what it is we really need to feel better.

Source works through us, not from outside of us because we are connected to Source, not separate. The more we understand this connection, the easier it is to be in the flow and union with our Source. Besides, since we always have a connection with Source, Source already knows what is best for us. One just needs to be in a positive, receptive place to receive what God or Source wants to bring to us.

Worrying About Our Past and Future

Ultimately, no one else can control what we think about, so it's our own decision if we choose to hold onto thoughts about the past. By focusing on thoughts of the past, we keep them alive and continuing to attract similar energies in our present moment. Pleasant memories are wonderful to reflect on, but if we focus on negative past events then we are keeping this negative energy active in our present life. At any given moment we can choose not to focus our attention on the past. Our minds create our experiences and perceptions of the world, so it is up to us to choose where we will focus our attention. The only real moment is now, and it is up to each of us to choose how we will define ourselves going forward.

Positive planning for our future in the now moment can pay off, but worrying about our future is counterproductive in regard to the law of attraction. We must remember that everything is ultimately energy, so worrying only works to create an energetic attraction to what we are worrying about! Instead of worrying, we can try dreaming or visualizing a positive and fulfilling future for ourselves and those we love. Even if there is something happening in our future and the outcome looks bleak, we can take action to help the situation as best as we can, but focus on a positive outcome for ourselves.

How the Law of Attraction Really Works

It all begins with a thought.

Now that we have looked at some of the mental blocks getting in the way of understanding and using the law of attraction, let's look at how it truly works. The metaphysical belief behind the law of attraction is this: One's true self is always part of and connected to Source (God, the Universe). Our Source is a loving energy consisting of wellbeing, goodness and infinite possibilities, and through our Soul's connection to Source, we have the ability to tap into and create infinite possibilities in our own lives. The only reason we do not receive the benefit of this infinite possibility is that we are blocking it; we are not allowing it to manifest beneficially in our lives.

We block this flow of abundance and opportunity through our negative thoughts of lack, fear, self-doubt and unworthiness. The law of attraction responds to our thoughts and feelings. It does not respond to what we say we want if what we want is different than how we feel.

Even if we say we don't feel lack or doubt or unworthiness,
it doesn't matter—the rational thought of that doesn't matter.
What matters is the true feelings we have underneath
the rational thought.

The law of attraction is universal, meaning it reaches all aspects of life on this planet and the non-physical realm as well. There is not a specific verbal language we must use or a ritual we must perform, nor is there a score keeper determining who is naughty and nice. If a person is in a positive oriented mindset toward getting what they want, then they are in alignment with the wellbeing of the Universe bringing it to them. If they are in the mindset of believing they are worthy of having whatever it is they want, then they are in alignment with the Universe bringing to them what they are worthy of feeling. If a person loves themselves and loves life, then they are in alignment with the loving nature of the Universe bringing loving experiences to them.

If a person has a negative attitude, focuses on lack, is angry or fearful, they are out of alignment with the Universe and creating a resistance to the flow of love, abundance and wellbeing it offers. We don't use the law, we get in alignment with the law and let go of our resistant thoughts. By quieting our minds and being positive, open-minded people, we get plugged in to the higher consciousness of Source. Source already knows what is best for us, we only need to align ourselves with receiving what Source always wants to give.

We all are different when it comes to how we believe things in life will manifest for us, but the law of attraction is steadfast. We all have our own filters. Some see God as bringing things into our existence while others believe this abundance comes from Source or the Universe. Ultimately, they all mean the same thing since we are all connected and one with everything.

Each of us who has this individualized life experience has the power to focus on what it is we want and bring it into our experience in this lifetime. It is beneficial to always remember that we are an aspect of Source and thus always connected to Source. The larger part of Source recognizes our feelings more fully when we align them with the good will of Source, which is our true nature.

The law of attraction does not respond to our negative and fearful energy by bringing us positive things to change how we feel. Instead, we change how we feel so that our feelings are in a more positive alignment with receiving more positive things in our lives. When using the law of attraction, we must always focus first on knowing that we are connected to all that is. Secondly, we must align our thinking with feeling the positive outcome of what it is we are seeking. This is the "plugging in the toaster to make toast" my teacher, Dr. Paul Masters, spoke of.

Source works through the Universe to bring into our physical existence the things that match the positive feelings we focus on.

The Power to Manifest

There is an excitement about knowing that we are part of this magnificent creative force we call the Universe, Spirit, God or Source. There is a comfort in knowing that we are worthy and knowing that we are not defined by our ego thoughts and our past ego actions. With this knowledge we easily exist in a higher conscious state of mind, a state of mind that makes it easy for us to feel secure and happy in our lives. Knowing this and feeling this make it so much easier to be in a positive place to manifest. When we have our down and depressed moments, we need to do everything we can to remember how magnificent we truly are—there is always so much joy and love in knowing that. Yes, the death of loved ones and tragedies of our human existence will still occur, but when we exist in a higher conscious state of mind we will be in a stronger mental space to handle them.

We do not attract tragedy into our lives from the Universe; Source only brings us wellbeing, so one should never feel they caused or attracted tragedy. We do, however, attract similar earthly energies, bringing people or scenarios into our lives that match our vibration, so the company we keep and the space we live in will likely be a reflection of our own selves.

A person exists in a higher conscious state of mind when they realize their thoughts and feelings carry a vibration and this vibration brings into their experience the things that match their vibration. It is through one's higher conscious thinking that a person realizes the need to clarify and quiet their ego thoughts so they can move beyond passively experiencing the always-present law of attraction and actually put it to work in manifesting what it is they want. To clarify the mind, we clean up our negative ego thinking, no longer focusing on low vibrational thoughts such as fear, judgement, anger and resentment. Instead, we focus on higher vibrational thoughts and feelings such as love, compassion, courage, hope and acceptance.

Through continual, conscious focus on higher vibrational thoughts and feelings, a person also eliminates negativity from the storehouse of thoughts held in their subconscious mind. This leads the subconscious to automatically communicate and respond with a more positive, higher vibration, which allows us to automatically receive and experience more beneficial outcomes in our lives.

The positively programmed subconscious attracts positive situations to our lives, which we aren't even consciously focusing on. This is called "being in the flow" or having doors just open for us along our journeys in life. We will know when we have obtained a positively focused subconscious mind because life seems much easier for us. This happens because we are creating less negative mental resistance to the positive flow of energy coming from the Universe, bringing forth the experience of wellbeing and ease.

This will not happen for the person who tries to manifest wants in their lives by entertaining positive thoughts and feelings about what they want, but continues to think negative or unworthy thoughts about other things in their lives. This type of thinking keeps the subconscious in a negative state and it will conflict with one's conscious focus to manifest. Existing in a higher conscious state of mind is having one's conscious thoughts and subconscious thoughts in positive alignment. It is necessary to have this positive mental alignment before beginning to manifest because the subconscious is a big factor in playing out our thoughts behind the scenes of our conscious thinking.

When a person exists in a higher conscious state of mind, they can successfully put manifestation to work in their lives.

While others who are ruled by ego struggle and stress to achieve what they want in life, the higher conscious person will reach their goals with ease and support from the Universe.

Manifesting is the art of bringing into our experience something we do not currently have. Since we do not currently have it, we must imagine what it feels like to have it and then focus on that feeling. By focusing our thoughts on the feelings of joy, satisfaction and happiness of having it already, we hold this vibration in our energy body. The energetic space we create to hold this "having" vibration is what tells our creative non-physical Source to bring the want into our experience.

Instructions for Manifesting Something Specific

In the following exercise, think about and reflect on what you want and write it down. Writing your wants down works as a visual reminder to constantly keep yourself mentally focused on what it is you want. Keep the list where you can see it; you could even put it on your phone or computer as a reminder, perhaps as a screensaver. It can take time for some things to manifest, so keep this list with you as long as you need. I keep my old lists as a beautiful reminder that everything I focused on manifesting in the past came to me.

✍Exercise: What are you wanting for your life?

➢**Part 1:** Make a list of your wants, be honest with yourself and do not hold back or judge yourself for wanting what it is you want. We will analyze the list later and possibly do some editing.

➢**Part 2:** Now go through the list and separate out material things from feelings and experiences.

⌘**For example:**

Material	Feelings	Experiences
New car	I want to feel secure	The ability to travel
Sapphire ring	I want to feel loved	To go sailing

➤**Part 3:** Now let's focus on editing your material list if needed. Focus on the reason you want the material things. Be honest with yourself here. If any of these material wants are due to feelings of inadequacy or the need to fit in, I highly recommend letting them go. There is absolutely nothing wrong with wanting things for yourself as long as they are for you to enjoy, but if you want them to change how you feel for ego reasons (looking desirable or having more than others), then they will not truly bring you fulfillment once you have them. You may enjoy a brief moment of joy and fulfilment by succeeding in getting what it is your ego wants, but then you will quickly go back to how you felt before receiving it. So, when looking at your list of material things, make sure they are things you truly want for your enjoyment or that they are things you need. All other material things are not worth focusing your attention on.

➤**Part 4:** Going forward, put your focus on the list of wants you created—the final, edited material list along with the feelings and experiences you listed. How will the material things make you feel when you have them? What will it feel like to experience what it is you wish to experience? Add these feelings to your list as well.

If it helps, take a small sheet of paper and write your list of wants along with how they will make you feel and keep the list with you. Use it as a reminder to focus on having what you want and how it feels to have it. When you think about how it feels to have what it is you want, think and feel as if you already have the experience or own the item in your current life. This good feeling of having already what you want is the basis of manifestation and going beyond passively experiencing the law of attraction. You create the vibration of "having," which then attracts other energy or things which vibrationally match what you feel you already have.

The higher consciousness of Source wants to bring you everything you desire and works endlessly to do so, but it's your field of energy or vibration that communicates the want.

Upon waking in the morning, try to focus your attention on what it is you want to feel for the day and visualize the positive outcomes you want to see happen. This helps program or guide our mental state of being to be in a positive state for the day, and it also programs the subconscious so that it will eventually automatically inspire you to be in a positive state upon awakening. It is important to do this in the morning because many of us like to think of what happened yesterday, such as a conversation or event that got our attention. A hundred good things could have happened yesterday, but it's likely some of us will find the one bad thing that happened and focus our attention on that. Focusing on yesterday keeps us in the energy of yesterday, and unless it was a phenomenal day, we need to release it and focus on creating our present moment and feelings.

Place your attention on what it is you are trying to manifest in your life and focus on how good it feels to have it. In fact, focus on feeling as if you already do have it. If it is something you have never had or experienced before, then you must imagine what it feels like to have it.

Throughout the day, try and remind yourself to become present in the moment and focus on being in a positive state of mind; if you were not already mentally there, then use affirmations or focus on something pleasing to get yourself there. Once you have achieved a relaxed and positive state of mind, move your awareness to focusing on the good feelings of what it's like to have what it is you are trying to manifest. Do this process as often as you can throughout the day and don't become discouraged if you go through a period of time where you forget to do it. Even if you forget for days on end, it doesn't matter; just get yourself back to the process of focusing your mind on feeling what it is you are seeking.

Consistent practice is the key. Remember, if you are staying in a positive mental state you will have programmed your subconscious to unconsciously manifest beyond your conscious awareness. The subconscious is a mental powerhouse working behind the scenes in a positive way to manifest, even if you consciously forget! The subconscious mind does not know whether you actually have what you are seeking or not, so even if you do not have it, your subconscious mind will work continuously to give off the energy of having it. This helps guide the energies of the Universe to bring into your experience the things that match the vibration of you having it. You do not need to understand the mechanics of how this works, just know your thoughts and feelings carry an energetic frequency and you have an energy body that holds them as a vibration (your vibe).

Visualization can assist in the manifestation process as well. Visualize yourself having what it is you are seeking. What does it look like? What does it look like in your life? A powerful visualization for manifesting what you want is to focus on your solar plexus chakra or your gut area and visualize pulling what you want to this area. While doing this, feel in your gut area what it feels like to have it. Your solar plexus is an entry point for your energy body and it is the seat of your subconscious mind (think "gut feelings").

If anyone tries to deter you from manifesting or makes you feel unworthy in the process, remember they are under the influence of ego and ignore their unaware and unawakened mind. Source, through the workings of the law of attraction, recognizes the positive energy or vibe you carry in your energy body. Source will work to bring into your existence that which matches the positive energy of that desire. There may be some missed connections along the way, but Source will not stop trying to create a path to get to you what you want.

Now, if you lay around on the couch all day watching television, it's going to be harder for Source to find a path because there is resistance in being inactive. For most, things do not magically appear, but I do not rule it out—miracles are possible in this Universe if you believe them to be.

If you are getting inspired to visit places, connect with others and create new ideas, then you are creating movement and Source is able to find more paths to get you what it is you seek. Always remember, manifesting is carrying the wonderful feeling of having what it is you are seeking. Once you have carried this wonderful feeling for a period of time, you subconsciously communicate this vibration, which assists in keeping you in positive alignment with the want and will create positive outcomes beyond your conscious awareness.

You can use whatever tools you like in assisting with this process, whether you meditate to move beyond resistant ego thinking or state affirmations to guide your conscious mind. Remember, it's your divine right to have the life you believe you are worthy of so don't give up. Believe in your ability to do this and make it fun!

Karma Explained

The concept of karma is tricky. Sometimes it may stand in the way of people believing fully in themselves and knowing they can become and manifest anything they want in this lifetime. I have heard many people say they are cursed in this lifetime, or that things appear to always go wrong for them because they have bad karma. I have also heard people say, "They must have done something really bad in a past life to have the karma and life they have now." I wonder if people really go through life thinking their life is destined to be bad, so they just expect it. How horrible if this were the case, since they would be creating a block to Source bringing them abundance and wellbeing?

The modern belief in karma as being some spiritual price to pay stands in the way of one's higher conscious growth because this view of karma is coming from an ego perspective. Karma is an older word for law of attraction; it's another word used to describe the cause and effect of the energy we carry, which comes from our thoughts and feelings. Now that we know how the law of attraction and manifestation works, we know non-physical universal energy responds or interacts with us when we are in a positive energetic alignment with it; there is not a higher power keeping tabs on one's ego deeds or actions.

I too used to believe karma was a real spiritual law that dictated each of our lives based on things we did in our current and past lives. As I progressed with my study of metaphysics and energy, not only did this idea seem out of alignment with the non-judgmental Universe and Source, it also didn't fit into the higher conscious understanding that ego does not transition to the Soul upon physical death. Through insight I receive from Source by being in a higher conscious state of mind, I realized that karma is not a real thing, karma is not a punishment, karma is not a reward, karma is just a word. Karma is a term created by humans, it is not a spiritual law; outside of our own human thoughts about karma, it does not exist. Karma translated from sanskrit (Indo-European language) means action, and in the case of human interaction, it could be used to describe the cause and effect energy exchange between people.

Most importantly, it's not a judgment of humans brought on by God, as some think. God, Source whatever it is we choose to call our non-physical source, does not keep a karmic record of what we do. Source sees and feels us when we are in alignment with its loving high vibration, and it only wants to bring good to us. Source does not even see our human actions, which we define as bad by our ego minds. Doing bad things or having bad thoughts happens in the vacuum of the illusion we have created here on Earth with our ego minds. Because ego (the illusion of a separate mind) does not exist in heavenly realms or non-physical existence, it is not recognized by Source. Only negative ego energies of this world will respond to the mental negativity we carry.

We can still use the word karma, but to use it we must understand the context in which the word should be used. Often, we have relationships and interactions with certain people that create a mental attachment we could refer to as karma. This can happen on an individual conscious level or on a collective conscious level.

For example, if a relationship goes south and there is much blame and animosity between two people, the blame one holds onto could be referred to as karma. Also, two ideologies at war can create a collective animosity and this could be called karma, but it's really just a mental focus of energy creating a negative or positive mindset. A mindset is the creation of a mental energy we choose to attach to a situation or person. This attachment can be loving, or it can be hateful, but it is a mental attachment we choose to create. We are not bound to one another through karmic ties. The only energy we are attached to, no matter the circumstance, is the energy of love that attaches us to Source. The reason it feels so good to love others is because the feeling of love resonates with our loving connection to Source.

As for those who like the idea of good karma, it's really just the belief one holds that they are deserving, which actually creates positive outcomes. The positive expectation or feeling itself is what creates the positive vibration, which in turn creates or attracts future positive benefit to oneself. Just like the idea of bad karma, good karma does not come from Source keeping a record on each of our good deeds. It comes from us alone. It's our conscious or unconscious decision to involve ourselves in holding onto the energy of good or bad thoughts.

As for actions between two people, if one chooses to hold onto negative feelings, then they choose to hold onto the negative energy of the situation. If, however, the other person chooses to not hold onto the feelings caused by the situation then they let go of the negative energy. Feelings are energy and this energy is held in our energy body, so it's our own conscious choice to hold onto these feelings or let them go.

Here's a story about Sally and Joe. Sally and Joe are dating. Then one day Joe catches Sally cheating. Joe is irate with Sally and can't forgive her, so they break up and Joe goes on holding onto the hurt and resentment he believes Sally caused him. Joe is creating a negative mindset for himself and this energy will need to be balanced because the negative energy he carries is keeping him out of positive alignment with Source. Hopefully he will balance his energy by eventually, forgiving Sally or letting go of the resentment he is holding onto.

On the other side of the coin, Sally in her own mind was done with Joe and had her own justified reasons for cheating on him. She thinks Joe is overreacting and she is glad the relationship is over. She moved on to another relationship and she no longer even thinks about Joe. By doing this, Sally holds on to no negative thoughts from what happened and is therefore not carrying any negative energy from the situation.

In another scenario, Sally may feel seriously upset that she hurt Joe and she may hold on to guilt for causing him pain. Sally would then carry the negative energy of the situation, and because she can't forgive herself, her energy would be unbalanced. If the energy is not balanced, then Sally may attract a relationship down the road that will match energetically to what she carries in her energy body. She may feel she deserves the negative experience of a future relationship and having this feeling may actually create a relationship that is negative. This is a result of her own beliefs, this is not a tit for tat karmic punishment laid out by the Universe or Source.

It's so important for all of us to understand that Source does not judge us as doing right or wrong. This belief is a human ego construct that goes back to an old way of governing people's actions before modern laws were created. As spiritual beings, we are above the contrast of right or wrong; the polarity of right and wrong is a human ego experience. So, there is no karma, it's just a word, a word used to describe energy created by the human ego.

If someone believes in karma or lives by it, then it's part of their reality and their life experience here on Earth and that is OK. On the other hand, if someone doesn't believe in karma, then it's not part of their reality. Regardless, there are energies caused by ego thinking that we choose to hold onto while we are here, but this energy does not traverse with us into Spirit. Souls do not carry karma or energy attachments created during human lives because Souls do not have egos. Upon transitioning to Spirit, ego stays here and so does any concept of karmic energy. If the energy of ego lingers with the Soul while it transitions into a non-physical awareness, then energies coming from Source help to release it.

We tend to think of ourselves as individual people having individual experiences, which makes it easy for human minds to believe in a concept such as karma. In reality, we are all extensions of the Spiritual collective of Source, which ultimately means we are all connected to and part of one source. This understanding makes the concept that karma exists beyond human perception obsolete.

The Source from which we come is always assisting in balancing our energy; it is only our own thoughts and focused awareness that keeps our energy unbalanced. The best thing we can do for ourselves and the human collective is to be happy and loving with ourselves. By existing in this state, we release our own negative energy and beliefs in separateness, which helps to balance ourselves and others. Ultimately, we are all one human collective; what each of us does or thinks affects all of us on a grander human scale.

Creation of One's Own Beliefs

Most of us are not raised with the option to choose our beliefs. Instead we are taught to believe as our parents or guardians do. Yet, if these beliefs do not suit us when we determine our own sense of self, we have the freedom to choose another. For some this may entail attending a different church or changing religions altogether, but many others will have the desire to seek a spirituality that is non-religious in nature. Spiritual seekers are drawn to a spirituality that not only makes sense to their modern experiences but can also fit into where science and physics are intellectually taking us. The relationship between science and spirituality is not contradictory, rather, the two are complementary. This allows us to move beyond the conflict that exists between science and religion. Moving beyond this conflict allows us to have a greater expansion in beliefs because we are open to exploring and combining more concepts, rather than having a one-sided perspective.

With our modern ability to network it is easy to connect with the many spiritual teachers who have found fulfilling belief systems for themselves and who wish to share with others why their belief system is beneficial. Most of these spiritual teachers have good intentions and beautiful ideas, but discernment is always needed since spiritual experiences tend to happen on a personal level and are interpreted by the mind-set of the person receiving or experiencing them. Even though these experiences are very real to the person having them, they may not translate to the truth of someone else's experience. Spiritual knowledge and experiences come to each person differently, so there is no one correct way to believe in an experience.

Spiritual teachers and guides can be very helpful in getting one started on a spiritual journey, but they are not always necessary as one progresses on a spiritual path. Teachers inspire a person where they currently stand in the now moment, so when a person experiences growth, expansion or changes in life, it's likely the need for a different teacher or experience will arise to meet them where they are now.

Many of my friends have been my spiritual teachers at one time or another, but there are also people I consider my spiritual teachers whom I have never met. I have found these teachers through interviews, books, the internet and schooling and I did not need to meet them to get the message or teaching they offered.

There is no need to follow any teacher verbatim; a person can take from teachers what resonates with them and discard the rest. If we come across a new spiritual concept that make us feel good or excited, then our intuition is telling us it's in alignment with our own truth. If the belief makes us feel anxious, confused or unhappy then it is out of alignment with our truth and needs to be disregarded.

For those who choose to come up with their own beliefs in spirituality, it should be regarded as a sacred and enlightening journey that one should also find enjoyable. No belief is worth having if it doesn't bring a person a sense of happiness and wellbeing.

Our spiritual beliefs should complement and inspire our own lives but also bring a sense of peace and loving acceptance to our individual journeys.

It is feeling good about our beliefs that leads us to feel good about ourselves and life in general. This is the best outcome any belief can bring us because it helps to bring us into a higher conscious state of mind, aligning us with the higher consciousness of

Source. This alignment will allow us to have spiritual experiences for ourselves and give us the ability to receive divine insight, which in turn strengthens and confirms our beliefs. The strengthening of our positive and loving beliefs helps bring us even more into alignment with our greater self or Source. More alignment could also be referred to as "coming closer to God," or as I prefer, closer to the will of Source.

The beliefs we develop and hold onto become our own personal reality, and our reality is what guides our experiences in this life. Because our beliefs are foundational to our life experience, it is best to choose a belief in a non-physical world that complements what we desire to experience in life.

For instance, if one wishes to live a life of wellbeing and abundance, then they can choose to believe in a Universe of wellbeing and abundance, for this is the best way to align oneself with the things they are seeking. There is no one true reality or belief for all people; if there were, we would all think with the same ego mind.

Spiritual beliefs are not necessarily truths; they are human perceptions trying to make sense of our spiritual existence. The real us, our Soul, knows the truth, while our ego tries to comprehend truth. But, the ego cannot know truth because the ego is a temporary human state of mind and not eternal. The human ego mind creates a vision of what the afterlife will look like based on the thoughts, beliefs and experiences we have on Earth. This essentially creates a conception of the Spiritual afterlife as a reflection of our earthly human experience. If having these beliefs feels good to you, then there is nothing different you need to do. However, if we are seeking a spiritual truth, we need to release the trappings of the human ego mind.

Realizing our own magnificence and connection with Source is so very important no matter what we choose to believe. Too many of us have been programmed to think we are insignificant and unworthy of Source and even less worthy of connecting with it. Because so many of us fear that God has a critical and judgmental mind, we worry that if we were to communicate with God by any means other than worship, we could be persecuted or condemned. Instead, we try to hide our true selves from God since many teachings have led us to fear that our own human existence is flawed, corrupt, sinful and insignificant, making us feel unworthy of a higher connection. This is not true!

Source wants to reach us, guide us and help us. Source wants to communicate love and support to us, we just need to move past the fear and belief that our Souls are separate from Source and instead know that we are eternally loved, accepted and part of Source.

We are powerful in our own right and we have the power to control what exists in our lives—seen and unseen. We are never victims of unseen forces, but we can become victims of believing in such forces.

Any person's chosen belief would greatly benefit from a sense of their connection and oneness with Source. Sometimes it takes quieting the ego mind to feel this connection, and how this connection feels can be difficult to explain because it is a sense of knowing. This sense of knowing cannot be learned in a book, so beliefs can sometimes be difficult to explain because they are felt. Yet in this knowing feeling, we realize our own magnificent part in the greater whole of everything; we feel our connection of love and wellbeing to the love and eternalness that is Source.

When one does experience the loving feeling of being connected to Source, they get a sense of what truth feels like. As for gleaning spiritual truths from others and our experiences, we all need to follow our gut feelings. We need to nourish and celebrate our beliefs because our beliefs represent our individual truths, but we need to be respectful by not pushing our beliefs onto others. We can all enjoy our journeys through our own beliefs and not worry about the different journey another chooses to take. When our beliefs resonate with truth, there will be plenty of people who will come forth and ask, and many who will hold similar beliefs to share our experiences with.

Beliefs are the foundation of our human experience and beliefs are what can get us through the difficult aspects of human life, but no matter what any of us believe, in the end of this life we all return to loving truth.

✎Exercise: What are your beliefs?

Beliefs are beneficial to our wellbeing. They inspire us, enlighten us and help pull us through our darkest days. Those who do not believe in Source or a loving God may focus on the ego-driven material world and may find themselves quite upset or bothered by everyday events. They may turn to television and news networks as the source for their beliefs and thus become focused solely on world events. Focusing on the human ego actions of this world can lead to a life of fear, anger and resentment, especially if one focuses primarily on negative stories or events.

Your beliefs dictate how a spiritual experience will happen for you. If you have a love for Jesus, it is very likely your experience of Source will come to you as Jesus. If you focus your belief on angels or deceased loved ones being around you, then this may be the experience you have. The higher consciousness of Source can only reach us through what we believe and know. This is why no belief is wrong or better than another—as long as the belief is loving. Ego mind can only make an attempt to interpret the wisdom and truth of Spirit and God. When your conscious awareness leaves this body, you will see how everyone's Soul is connected to, part of and loved by God no matter what you believe or don't believe.

➤**Part 1:** What are your spiritual beliefs? Do you believe in an afterlife? If so, what does this look like to you?

➤**Part 2:** What spiritual concepts resonate with you? Write a list of a few spiritual concepts that intrigue you and then research them. You don't have to read a whole book, you can find snippets and articles on-line.

⌘**For example:** *Do you believe that the loved ones in your life who have passed surround you? There are so many books about this topic, do some research and get a book if you feel drawn to it.*

Do you mostly believe in Science? Look into quantum physics and spirituality. You will be amazed about how much the two intersect. It's a fascinating subject.

Do you believe in angels? There are so many inspiring books and writings on this topic, too.

Look into what inspires or intrigues you. Take from it what resonates with you and discard the rest. Discernment is key because everyone has their own perceptions, so everyone's spiritual experience will differ to a degree or more.

Beliefs begin with learning and they will help build a foundation for you. Beliefs are a journey and it is OK to allow them to constantly shift and grow. Writing out what you believe helps you to make more sense of your beliefs. It may surprise some people when they think they believe strongly in something but can't bring the belief together enough to even explain it in their writing.

Be proud of your beliefs, they are yours to have and experience. Don't let anyone tell you they are wrong or inferior. We all have different experiences in this lifetime so even people who experience the same teaching of a belief will have varying perceptions of what it means.

Chapter 7

Expanding Our Beliefs Through Higher Consciousness

Connecting to the higher consciousness of Source is an ability we all innately have because we come from and are part of Source. But this connection does not happen through our ego thinking; instead it happens by getting our own minds into a higher conscious state of awareness. By quieting our thoughts or focusing on loving feelings, which are high vibrational, we bring our minds into an awareness that aligns us with Source. It is through this alignment that we allow ourselves to receive what it is Source wants to communicate or bring to us.

I used to wonder why our bibles and religious writings talked about our ancestor's spiritual experiences, divine communications and miracles when none of these things seem to occur today. It made me feel as if we were left to our devices, abandoned or forgotten. I also felt that perhaps we were being tested, judged and kept in the dark, waiting for the return of some biblical event that would hand us our fate.

It wasn't until I began my own spiritual journey that I realized miracles, divine intervention, divine insight, wisdom and the eternal loving support of Source are always with us, and not only with us but always a part of us. It was not that we were ever forgotten or being tested; we were instead trained over time through our own human devices to fall asleep and forget our own divine connection to Source. We learned to fear that developing our own communication and connection to God was wrong and that we should only trust an authority chosen by a religious institution.

Over time, this led much of humanity to completely ignore or quickly shut down any recognition of our own personal divine connections and communications with Source. We closed our eyes to our own divinity and we fell asleep. We forgot that our Soul is wholly perfect and who we truly are while in this physical body. Yet Source has always been behind the human experience, and while we are in our physical bodies we are connected to Source through our Souls' connection. Source is always aware of our human self; we just have a tendency to shut Source out of our own minds on a daily basis.

When we let go of fearing our Source and instead begin recognizing ourselves as being a loving part of it, we more easily move into our own higher conscious state of mind and we awaken. We do not bring something to our life that wasn't already there, but now we are awake and able to feel and listen to what has always been present. It is through this awareness that we allow ourselves to more fully receive from the higher consciousness Source.

We can define aspects of what makes up our spiritual components, but ultimately, they are all connected to and part of the larger whole of Source. The collective of higher consciousness is infinitely intelligent, pure goodness and love. These are traits we as humans seek and admire because they are our true nature. When we become mentally aware of the realms of higher consciousness as part of our own existence, we become aware of our own greater selves and we feel the loving goodwill, security and reassurance this awareness brings to our minds. So, when we quiet our thoughts and bring ourselves into a higher conscious state of awareness, we can sense our Soul and our inner connection to Source. Through our intuition we can receive answers and guidance, which is always in our best interest and our greatest good.

Why is it always in our best interest? Because it's not coming from someone else's agenda, it's coming from the larger part of who we are, meaning that ultimately, it's coming from our own higher-knowing selves.

When a person discovers how to exist in a higher conscious state of awareness, it becomes easy for them to detect when they go back to functioning through human ego thoughts. Yes, reverting to ego thoughts will happen, even for the most consciously aware people. We are, after all, human and living in a world created by ego illusions. However, by being able to catch ourselves when we fall back into the pattern of our ego thoughts, we are able to choose not to entertain them. Understanding the difference (dualism) in our quality of thinking is crucial to maintaining balance and staying connected with the higher consciousness of Source.

If we could not recognize when we are solely functioning through our unbalanced and negative ego thinking, then we would continue to be victims of attracting other negative ego energies that match our own vibration. It is in all of our best interests to align our

thinking with the wisdom and loving thoughts of higher consciousness and not get lost in our uncertain and frail ego mind. The ego
is what creates the mental experience of separateness, but our connection to higher consciousness brings security and peace of mind.
We can absolutely live in this world of ego illusions and also exist
in a higher conscious state of mind—in fact, it becomes a beautiful
experience!

When receiving wisdom and insight from the higher consciousness of Source first begins, it often happens through one's imagination. This can be confusing because most of us believe our imagination is ours alone. In reality, our imagination is connected to the
higher consciousness of Source. Yes, our imagination can be influenced by our human experiences and programming, but this part of
imagination represents one's own ego fantasies or fears, which we
may consciously choose to dwell on.

It is the positive creative ideas, loving wisdom and guidance
that are coming from Source. We can understand the difference because the ego imagination typically is inspired by day-to-day things
happening in our lives—the programming we are exposed to—while
insight coming from Source is above and beyond our ego thoughts.

When someone wants to be inspired or guided, they can connect with the higher consciousness of Source while in a relaxed or
meditative state. Because we are connected to Source and not truly
separate, we can share our thoughts with our Source. To connect
with Source, we need to be mentally relaxed so that our ego mind
isn't running through its analysis of everything we need to do and
everything wrong with the world, etc. To achieve this mentally relaxed state, we can be still, or we can be moving. Sometimes doing
something physical helps to relax us, such as walking, hiking, practicing yoga, kayaking—it doesn't matter what the activity is as long

as it assists in stepping into the present moment and calming the mind.

When insight comes from Source, it is inspiring, loving and calming; it brings with it a sense of wellbeing. The quality of the thought is high vibrational, and it has a more loving quality than our ego thinking. As we have discussed previously, if you sense that you are receiving creative inspiration, take a moment to pause and write it down. Sometimes it's a flash of an idea; because it is not something we are consciously focusing on with our ego minds, it's easy to forget. Just like a friend telling us something, if we don't rehash what they said, we may forget the details.

This flash of insight could be something little or it could be an idea that could change our lives. It could be the next hit book, song or business idea or it could be an overwhelming urge to look at a hurt in one's life from a higher perspective, allowing one to mentally move past it.

Sometimes insight comes through in a larger message, and in this case it's essential to grab a pen and paper and start writing. There is no need to judge or analyze what is being written, just allow the inspiration to flow without the resistance of self-doubt and continue writing what comes into the mind. Later, a person can read the insightful message back to see how it flows, correcting grammar and such if they choose to. If the message is conditional, judgmental or negative, then they were allowing their ego mind to influence the insightful message. If it is loving, unconditional, inspiring and insightful, then it was indeed a message coming through their higher conscious connection to Source.

Pay attention to whether the message was written in the first person "I" or the second person "you." In some instances, one's writing may start out by saying "I" and then switch to "you." This is quite common. In my experience, I often begin writing in first person (I) and then as I relax and become less aware of my ego, my writing shifts into second person (you) as Source inspires my writing. For example, I may start out writing, "I need to do this." Later, after rereading it, my writing may have switched to something like: "You are ready and capable of making changes in your life."

The higher consciousness of Source does not connect with us to tell us what to do. If a person sees commands in their writing, they are coming from their own ego mind. However, if you are mentally seeking advice, Source will provide guidance that is in your best interest. Pay attention to the quality of the message. Does it feel like advice or a command? Advice feels good to receive, commands do not feel good to receive. Also, Source is non-conditional, meaning it's not judging our human existence, so if there is any type of judgement in what was written it is definitely not coming from Source.

When it comes to receiving insight from Source, we can only detect the vocabulary and terminology we already understand. Source does not communicate through our chosen human language, instead it uses paths of energy to reach us. These paths of energy do not hear us speak, they feel the vibration of our thoughts, and feelings—even our words carry a vibration. The higher consciousness of Source translates vibrational energy into thoughts that come into our imagination or creative mind. Because the message originates from energy or vibration, a person must have the vocabulary and ability to conceptualize the message in order to interpret it. If a person has very little knowledge and a limited vocabulary, then the way the message is interpreted will be just as limited. It does not mean the message will not be beautiful or will have less impact on a person; it just means the message meets a person where they are. There is a wisdom to the way the words are used and there is a loving feeling one receives when they read back a written insight.

With spiritual knowledge, a person can begin to understand that ultimately, we all are connected to and part of Source. Yet, we are taught and thus programmed as humans to perceive and understand things as separate. So, it is OK if a person perceives a message or a vision as coming from a deceased loved one, a past religious figure, an angel or another type of loving being. It is all in what one is comfortable with. Source detects the energy of our beliefs and works with what we believe to bring us guidance and inspiration.

There are some energies coming from Source that some people may refer to as "non-physical beings" because this energy feels new to a person. These energies may present themselves to those who have awakened and have an open mind by providing a name or definition of their purpose, but a name is only for us to use in reference to their energy, and it's all originating from Source. The energies coming from Source take on a name or characteristic for the purpose of the human audience; they do not truly have egos and personalities. They do have traits, but they relate to energy and not human characteristics.

An energy that presented itself to me refers to itself as a non-physical collective of wisdom coming from Source. This was not something I was taught existed, so it was something I was able to allow myself to perceive through my own spiritual growth. Before, I never realized there were collectives of knowledge energy in the non-physical realm. It is odd to explain because this is beyond most of our human ego understandings, but there are energies that relate to each of us and they want to help us in ways we can understand. This collective of wisdom coming from Source also helps to balance human physical energy with our Souls' energy. It is, of course, always helping me balance my energy as well. It's exciting to see what guides Source sends us and it's a beautiful experience when we connect with them. Life becomes so much more fascinating and worth living when we know we have so much assistance and that this life is a beautiful experience our Source wished us to have.

This process of how each of us chooses to receive spiritual insight is up to us as individuals. For example, some prefer having "knowing" thoughts come into their mind, while others receive insight through writing. There are also many divination tools people can use to help in connecting to higher consciousness, particularly in the beginning when practicing how to recognize our connection. All we need to do is find what method resonates with us as our truth; it does not matter what others do or use. There is no one way to connect with the higher consciousness of Source, the methods are as varied and different as we are.

I wish for all people who are ready to let go of the fears they have been programmed with and have the courage to allow themselves to connect mentally to what they are already part of. We can choose to listen to the loving guidance given to us from Source and receive help from the guides (energies) Source sends us, or we can rely on the ego, which does not always know what is in our best interest and can lead us down the wrong path in life. The ego is not an eternal part of Source and does not know truth; it can only try and make sense of the illusions it experiences.

How to Connect with Higher Consciousness

Sitting Alone with Oneself

Sitting alone with oneself is not meant to be a time to sit and go through the constant banter in one's mind such as, "What needs to get done?" "What will I wear to the party?" "What did my friend mean by what they said?" "I need to go on a diet, when should I start?"

It's also not meant to be the time when we create our to-do list. Sitting alone with oneself starts by letting go of the ego self-talk and really checking in with how we are mentally and physically doing. Physically, we need to take time to see if our bodies are tense, are we clenching our jaws or tightening our shoulders? Maybe we have been sucking in our stomachs or slouching, making our backs hurt. It's surprising how we create daily bad habits of positioning our bodies, which go unnoticed until we start to feel aches and pains.

Checking in on our breathing is also important. If our breathing is short or shallow, we need to focus on breathing deeply and relaxing the body while doing so. By taking deep calming breaths we oxygenize the body, revitalizing our cells and assisting with physical healing. Deep breathing also relaxes the body and helps to bring us into a physically relaxed state.

Mentally, we need to ask ourselves if we have been worrying too much about something or holding on to a grievance we need to let go of or forgive. This is a good time to remind oneself what this life is all about and who we truly are. All the emotional and stressful things we carry are just an ego experience, and no matter what is going on in our physical lives, our true selves are eternally safe and loved.

It can be difficult to release some troubling or worrisome thoughts when they are fresh in our minds, but we should at least try and give ourselves a moment of peace. We can always go back later to mulling over our issues. Better yet, we can try and connect with the higher consciousness of Source to assist in finding a solution and take action to resolve them. It is beneficial during this process of acknowledging our grievances to imagine breathing in calming and soothing energy and exhaling negative thoughts or energy.

When we are in a relaxed state, taking a moment to meditate is very beneficial to our wellbeing. If a person is not interested in meditating, they could have a mindful moment. A mindful moment could consist of appreciating anything we find beautiful around us or thinking thoughts of gratitude for the blessings in our life. Everyone is different, so a person can use any mindful method as long as it helps get them into a peaceful state of being and they are able to use the method daily. Taking a moment to sit with oneself and "check in" does wonders for a person.

☙Exercise: Deep breathing to check thoughts & emotions

Begin with taking slow deep breaths. If you haven't taken a deep breath in a long time it can actually make you cough and possibly make your heart temporarily race. It seems so simple, yet so many of us forget to breathe deeply, and some of us just don't realize how important deep breathing is. It awakens the body and makes a person's cells tingle, and if we haven't done it in a while it may take a second for the body to adjust. If you have initial negative sensations from deep breathing, don't give up, they will subside because deep breathing is part of our natural state of breathing.

Next, focus your attention on your body and check in on your arms and legs, your chest, stomach, shoulders and face. Are you clenching your jaw or your shoulders? Are you sucking in your stomach? If so, consciously go through and relax all parts of your physical body that are uptight or clenched. Breathe deeply as you allow your muscles to release and the tension to fade. Focus on relaxing all parts of your body, one at a time.

Please note: If you realize you are unable to take deep breaths and feel persistent discomfort, please see a medical doctor. We need to pay attention to how our bodies feel because they tell us when something might be wrong.

After you have relaxed your body you can check in with your thoughts and emotions. How do you feel right now? How have you been feeling lately? If you are feeling like everything is all good emotionally and you are happy and at peace, then you are ready to move on to practicing meditation or having a mindful moment (exercise on pg. 156).

If instead you feel depressed, fearful, anxious or unsettled, as so many of us do every day, first acknowledge that you are having these feelings and then begin to address them. It's OK to have these emotions—you're human and we all experience them. It is not OK to hold onto them.

So many of us don't want to acknowledge our emotions, especially if they are negative, but nevertheless our emotions are telling us something. Not only do our emotions speak to us about our state of being, they are also energy that can influence our physical bodies as well as our energy body and our connection to Source. As we have discussed, ego energy attracts other like ego energy, so if you are experiencing an emotion (energy) you don't want, then you need to acknowledge it, or you will continue to experience situations and people that match that energy.

Please know I am talking about attracting daily feelings and instances of life, I am not talking about attracting tragedy. Tragic situations happen to us all, no matter what our mindset is. You can be a saint and still have the experience of losing an innocent child. While we are here on Earth we will all experience tragedy and sadness. I feel it's irresponsible to tell someone that they are experiencing loss or tragedy because they attracted it to themselves. Tragedy and sadness will happen no matter what, for these experiences are part of life on Earth; it's how we understand and deal with the tragedies in life that matters.

After you have acknowledged your emotions, look a little deeper to what caused the emotions. Was it a person or a recent event that caused the emotion? If it's something or someone from the past who is no longer part of your current life, please know you are in a safe place now and the situation or person can no longer harm your wellbeing. Whether the cause of the emotion was in the past or present, you can now consciously release it from your life and let the energy of the situation go. If you need to, forgive yourself or the cause, because ultimately, we either choose to carry the energy from the situation or release it through forgiveness.

You do not have to forget what the event or person caused, but you can let go of the power it has over you and release all the energy attached to it. If this distressing event is still an ongoing situation or comes from a person in your current life, focus your attention on how you can change the situation or remove yourself from the person causing you grief. Connecting with the higher consciousness of Source can help provide guidance and the energy to make a change for the better in your life. Try your best not to focus on being a victim or holding on to the belief that "this situation is just how life is for me." Life does not have to be difficult, and it shouldn't be. We are not here to suffer.

Forgiveness and Why It's So Important

Forgiveness can be difficult. You may have some trouble with the previous exercise if you have not been able to forgive others or yourself for things that happened in the past. Unfortunately, not being able to forgive yourself or others will keep you in an ego state of mind, which is out of alignment with Source. Forgiving and moving past negative emotions allows you to mentally exist in a higher conscious state of mind that aligns you with Source. This alignment allows for the positive attributes of abundance and goodwill to flow more easily into your life experience.

If you experienced a grievance in the past, it is only your current awareness keeping it alive in the present moment. The past no longer exists except for what you choose to hold onto and replay in your mind, so by forgiving, you remove your focus from the grievance and it no longer exists in your reality. It may have had an impact on who you are today. If you like who you have become (if, for instance, you can say you are stronger and wiser from the experience), then thank the experience for at least that. But choose to release the negative energy of the situation.

If you blame who you have become today on the situation, then you are holding yourself in place and not allowing yourself to grow beyond the experience. At any time in one's life, they may choose to liberate themselves from victimhood and see that it does not have to hold them to a life they do not want to have.

People who commit wrongdoings are lost in ego; they do not see from a higher perspective that when they hurt someone else, they are also hurting themselves. This hurt is a result of being out of perpetual alignment with Source and when this happens, life for them is more difficult and challenging—a life of suffering. When they get themselves into this difficult negative cycle, they are more prone to act out and attack because they erroneously blame the world and those around them for the misfortunes they are in fact creating for themselves. But, you do not have to join them in their experience of misery. Wrongdoing from others is not "judged" by God, but due to the law of attraction, what a person gives off energetically, they will attract in turn.

If you are currently dealing with a negative situation in your life, then you need to find a way out. You can't change a person who doesn't understand how they are lost in ego thinking. If their actions cause you grief or exhaust you, then focus your attention on getting away and finding a better circumstance for yourself. (For the purpose of manifestation, focus on what you want to be and feel, not on the grief they are causing you.) If someone causes you pain and grief and you allow it because they have created a story of being a victim to make you feel sorry for them, then walk away! It is not your responsibility to fix them. It is manipulative of them to make excuses to draw your sympathy while at the same time they continue with their bad behavior and actions. They are not your responsibility, they have their own path and issues to work through but not at the expense of your happiness and wellbeing.

Look to higher consciousness for guidance in situations involving others and yourself. Learn to recognize the lessons these life experiences bring and heal yourself by letting go of them through forgiveness.

I know forgiveness is easier said than done, but you can do this! Realize your greater true self and the greater self of the person with whom you had the interaction. You are both divine aspects of Source having a sometimes-imperfect ego human experience, and we all have been programmed with certain human ways of reacting. It's likely that if a person lashes out, they are carrying a tremendous amount of resentment and hurt. Have compassion for the pain people carry, but do not let them back in your life if they refuse to realize their pain and get help. No other person is your responsibility to fix. Focus on healing any hurt or resentment you may be carrying. That will do more good for the world than exhausting yourself by trying to fix the way others choose to perceive their lives.

If the ill feeling action was caused by your own accord, then focus on trying not to repeat what you did. Remind yourself, if and when the situation happens again, that you will have an opportunity to handle this new situation in a way that is more compassionate and understanding. Most importantly, forgive yourself. If you are acting out, then you are likely carrying some type of pain yourself. By finding the cause of this inner pain, you can work to forgive or release the source of it, even if it happened fifteen years ago! I promise you will feel better by letting the negativity of the situation go because you will lift your mood and get back in positive alignment with Source.

✍Exercise: Letter writing to bring forgiveness

Write a letter to someone who caused you distress or to a negative situation that you need to release from your thoughts through forgiveness. If you are using a journal, write this letter on a separate piece of paper, or if using a computer, make sure you can print it. Write the letter as if you are going to send it, but do not hold back. They will never see the letter. This letter is not for them or the event, it is for you. Describe how the person or event hurt or wronged you and also how or why they/it can no longer hurt or wrong you.

End the letter by focusing on finding the greater meaning to this life experience by seeing the situation through a higher perspective and not through the limited ego mind. The ego mind will just keep reminding you of how hurt you are and how the person or situation is unforgivable. Through a higher perspective you can see how the experience was an illusion of this world, and that the true you can never be hurt. This is because your Soul is not hurt from the experience, only your ego is hurt.

Now, symbolically release the energy and emotion brought up by writing this letter by burning it. If you can't burn it, then bury it or throw it away. Any residual energy you hold onto from this situation needs to be released, and burning the letter is a powerfully symbolic way of releasing it.

The process of writing is cathartic because it helps to bring forth and acknowledge emotions you may not even realize are affecting you. The action of burning the letter or throwing it away is a powerful symbolic gesture that you no longer hold onto the emotion of the experience.

Forgiveness can be tough, but the pain we carry as a result of holding on to our grievances can be debilitating to our wellbeing and energy. If you struggle with forgiveness and letting go, there are many guides, counselors and coaches willing to help. If you can't afford them, try the lessons of *A Course In Miracles*. The lessons of *ACIM* are free and they will teach you how to move past pain and resentment and take control of how you feel. Spend your thought energy on making a change and getting assistance if you need to, but please don't stay focused on accepting any situation that is causing you grief.

When you find yourself at peace, not only will you be better able to enjoy a deeper meditation or mindful moment, you will also feel physically better by letting go of thoughts that are a source of stressful energy in your body.

Meditation

✤Exercise: Create a sanctuary for yourself

If you can find a space in your home, designate a room for quiet relaxation or meditation. Keep in this space ambient lighting or candles, plants, fountain, essential oil diffuser, crystals, art, notebooks, writings or anything inspirational. Create a comfortable place to sit or even lounge in the room. Use this space to meditate daily if you can. If you cannot get into meditating, then focus on your breathing, relaxing the body and having a mindful moment. You could also work with your affirmations in this space, and it's also a great space to write down any messages coming from Source. These messages may come as inspirations or other insights when you are in a peaceful state of mind.

If you choose, it's OK to tell others they are not allowed into this space because this room will hold a special energy for you. You will create an energy in this space that is high vibrational, uplifting and healing to you. It will also become a place for balancing, rejuvenating and cleansing your energy to create peace, inspiration and serenity in your life.

If you live in a full house and there is no space for this, try and find a corner of a room, a basement area or even attic space to make your own. You can make an unfinished space serene and calming. If you have young children, try and find a schedule where you can take a moment for yourself in your own space, perhaps during their nap time. Or, introduce your children to the space and teach them the importance of it.

✥Exercise: Learning to Meditate

Meditation is a tool to benefit your mind and relax the body more deeply because it allows your ego mind to completely get out of the way and allow the spiritual life force energy that comes from Source to heal, balance, center, revitalize and ground your energy.

When your body is in a relaxed state and you are sitting comfortably, you can try and bring your focus into a meditative state. If you choose, you may listen to a fountain, nature sounds, gentle music or white noise to help calm your mind or drone out any noise around you. When you feel ready, close your eyes and take several deep breaths. At first you may notice how thoughts keep coming into your mind's awareness. The ego mind will repeat thoughts over and over, play the last song you heard in your head or sometimes over-analyze something going on in your life. You can go back to analyzing and singing songs in your head later, but now, for a short time, allow yourself the amazing benefit of total peace of mind.

The key is not to try and eliminate your thoughts. Rather, remove your attention from them. In the beginning you will be aware of thoughts coming into your mind, but practice not giving them your attention. As your thoughts arise, you can imagine them as bubbles of thoughts coming up in your head. As these bubbles of thought arise, pay no attention to them. If you allow the bubbles to just float by, they will dissipate back into a place of unawareness. As with anything, the ability to let your thoughts go takes patience and some time to develop, but please do not become discouraged. If you find yourself struggling, create a mantra. Mantras are tools used to distract one's focus from a thought. They work best when they do not make any sense or trigger another thought. I don't often use a mantra but when I do, I prefer to use a phrase such as "Love and

Light." I do not focus on what it may mean, I just focus on stating the phrase.

You can come up with your own mantra or search online for some examples, but for now, let's try using my mantra as an example. As your thoughts arise, do not focus your attention on the thought; instead, state silently in your mind the phrase "Love and Light." Do not think about the idea of what the phrase means; instead focus your attention on saying the phrase and breathing deeply. By repeating your mantra every time you begin to focus on a thought, you will eventually train your mind to not focus on a thought coming into your awareness. In time, you will be able to sit in peaceful silence and not think thoughts nor rely on a mantra.

Let's say, for example, while you're sitting in silence a song keeps popping into your head. State silently to yourself, "Love and Light." If the song is still popping into your head, continue to state to yourself, "Love and Light." If the song keeps repeating in your head, then keep saying your mantra with the intention of not focusing your mind on the thought or song. It doesn't matter if you are practically chanting "Love and Light" at first. Don't worry, this method works! Eventually the thoughts stop coming and you no longer need to use the mantra. At this time, you slip into the meditative state, which is relaxing, peaceful and beyond our thoughts. It's a mind-training process and eventually you will find yourself in a silent meditative state in which Source is able to connect more fully with you and through you. This Spiritual connection is a natural and automatic process; you do not have to do anything else.

Try to meditate for twenty-five to thirty minutes daily, but in the beginning just try as long as you can—even two to three minutes to start, then move to five minutes and continue to move up from there. It does not take a long time to connect Source more fully with your body and mind through the inner connection of the Soul. In just a little time, Source can assist in healing the energy of the mind and body and bring forth creative inspiration and wisdom. Source knows what is best for you, you just need to get your resistant ego thoughts out of the way and allow this natural process to happen.

With the practice of meditation, you will feel relaxed, rejuvenated, grounded and less stressed. But, something else really beautiful happens—you begin to realize that your true self is not the constant banter in your mind! These repeating thoughts are your ego mind doing what it does best, but it is not the true you! Your true self is peaceful, loving and connected, and when you meditate you will begin to recognize this. There is a greater spiritual you here to experience this existence and you have an ego mind or filter you can learn to control.

When we do finally realize our true nature, we then realize that the true us is never hurt, damaged or anxious. These feelings and emotions are just ego experiences that we are carrying through this lifetime, but we don't have to carry them! We can choose to release the energy of the experience by changing our perspectives in any given moment. This is perhaps one of the greatest things meditating has helped me to understand.

Connecting with Source Through Nature

Meditation is a sure way to get our own minds in alignment with the higher consciousness of Source, but being in nature is another effective method. Nature does not exist in an ego mental state, so it is the purest form of Source here on Earth. Yes, we assign our own ego meaning to what nature is, but that does not define it. Nature has purpose and instinct, but it is open to the creative forces of Source. Nature allows the energies from Source to work through it and express itself without the limitations of an ego mind.

When humans who are under the influence of an illusory ego mind come into nature, they feel the presence of Source, which feels good. They may not know why it feels so good, but they do know it relaxes their minds, invigorates and inspires. The trees, the flowers, the mountains, streams and oceans—they touch all of us with their majesty and serenity. Those who see through a higher conscious perspective feel nature's pure representation of Source through their inner Soul connection. This brings them into alignment with Source on a mental level. Yet, being in nature is beneficial to all, grounding our energy by balancing us and bringing us a sense of wellbeing.

Technology has brought us access to vast resources of information that allow us to expand our minds and learn much more about our world, yet it has a tendency to take us away from nature. The awakened have found ways to incorporate technology into their lives that are respectful to their connection with nature. They do this by balancing time spent watching television, being on the computer and playing digital games by being in nature and having mindful moments. Unfortunately, those who have not awakened spend too much of their time playing video games, binge watching television and keeping themselves pent up in indoor spaces. They tend to have an indifferent attitude toward nature or may even see it as a nuisance that needs to be manicured, cut down and replaced by shopping centers and other places used to satisfy the human ego. Many would much prefer a mall, water park, zoo or movie theater to a place of nature because they need constant stimulation to distract themselves from their own relentless ego thoughts.

The quiet, peaceful solitude of nature is not as effective if a person cannot stop themselves from thinking and looking at their phones. I'm sure we have all seen the people who cannot stop talking while walking or hiking in nature because they do not know how to quiet their minds. Luckily, even those who are spiritually asleep feel some benefit from nature. They may describe it as fresh air and exercise or feel good about visiting a place that preserves animal life, but they are feeling some unaware connection to Source in nature as well. Thank God some of those who are asleep have some reverence for nature, because if they didn't, there would not be many natural places left.

While nature is grounding and healing, many of us are not able to get into it as often as we would like. But, there are tools people can use to focus their minds on spiritual healing. Instruments of sound, touch and even certain physical movements assist in aligning oneself with the beneficial energies of Source. The number of tools and methods to do this are so numerous and diverse that it's really up to us as individuals to find what resonates with us. It doesn't matter if others think it's strange or silly; what matters is that we have an attraction to use a specific tool or method and we use it with the intention of connecting to Source to receive healing. I have found yoga, crystal healing bowls, qigong, walking, massage and even swimming to be tools to help me connect to Source. It really has to do with our intentions. When we find something relaxing or calming to our mind, we can assign our intention to it. In doing so, our intention will assist us in connecting with Source.

Any tool can be assigned with a beneficial meaning, and your purpose for using the tool does not have to be healing. What the tool really does is help us to focus our awareness on our connection to Source, and in doing so bring ourselves into a higher conscious state of awareness in order to receive what Source wants to provide.

Chapter 8

Higher Consciousness Is Ours

Everything is connected and ultimately an aspect of Source and its creation. This world we live in is all made of vibrating energy that ebbs and flows. Energy through the experience of Spirit comes together in a perfect orchestration with nature to create all living things, thus all living things have an aspect of Source inhabiting them. Many people are asleep and experiencing life solely through ego, while other people are awake and aware of their spiritual nature. Humans are unique in that we are trained into ego thinking and as a result we have to awaken from its grasp to connect to Source.

When a person awakens, they not only discover their ability to receive creative inspiration and guidance from Source, they also begin to understand their ability to receive life force energy, which is healing and balancing to the body. The awakened person often allows this natural process of receiving life force energy to happen while they are in a meditative or mindful state. With their ego mind out of the way, they create a non-resistant path for this natural connection to happen through their Soul or inner connection to Source, which allows them to receive it.

Messages from the Wisdom of Source

Following are some examples of messages that come to me from the higher consciousness of Source—especially when I am experiencing nature, meditating and as I engage in my writing practice. These messages come as sudden insights, and the difference for me is obvious because they are not typical of my daily ego thinking and interactions.

You Are All Those Things

Have you ever looked in the mirror and wished you were someone different? Perhaps you felt you could be better or greater than you are now? You may have at one time or another asked God or Spirit, "Why am I not perfect?" "What did I do to have this body or to have this life?" But, what if—for a moment—you could be all knowing by stepping into the mind of God or Spirit? Would you be surprised to discover that God and Spirit are in fact you as well? Would it blow your mind to discover you are not separate from them or anything else, for that matter?

The experiences you are having are also experiences they are having. So why would they want you to think or experience anything less than the best, since they are you? Everyone is connected; no one is separate. Nothing real, outside of you or beyond you says that you are less than or that you must suffer. Your beliefs and perceptions are the illusions that lead you to feel you are less than perfect. The reality is that your life and your awareness are all part of the reality of God and Spirit. You are neither alone nor separate from them or anything else here on Earth.

So, knowing you are one with God, one with Spirit, one with everything that is magnificent and beautiful, why waste any more time feeling any less than? Instead, be certain you are one with everything beautiful, abundant and successful. Whether you can see it now or not it is OK, but this is your TRUE reality. You just need to believe it and claim yourself to be the magnificent creation you are. Enjoy every part of your being, for you are perfection, you are part of God and all of creation. You can never truly be anything else but wholly loved and accepted as a magnificent piece in the beautiful tapestry we call the Universe. Know you are one with all that is; know you are always a beautiful, perfectly made piece to this puzzle and know you can be and feel anything you wish. The Universe loves you, God loves you, and your Spirit loves you because they are you! So, now will you join them in loving yourself? When you love yourself, you love them. For what they truly ARE, and what you truly ARE, is the love and the light of creation.

You Want to Be Here!

You choose to be here, you want this experience. This is a beautiful world; this world is not a mistake. It may be hard at times to see this world as the beautiful world it is when what you see looks so angry, upset and even murderous. This is what so many are being programmed to see and experience, but it is not the truth of this world.

Many have been trained out of understanding that they have the mental creative power to make this life a beautiful experience for themselves. There are many Souls who have wished to uplift and inspire a family that has lost its will to live and has given up on having a beautiful life. The Soul knows it can do this, and can see a path to doing it. But once the Soul is immersed in the ego programming of the family or community, it has a hard time not falling into its illusions. Many, many Souls come to this experience to try and change thinking and uplift humanity, to help them see a beautiful world instead of a world of attack and fear. If humanity could collectively awaken, if they could collectively change their minds about how they want to see and experience this world, then the true, beautiful reality of this world could be experienced.

As it is now, the ego illusions have a firm grip. But each awakening Soul will continue to try and do its part to inspire, brighten and lift the human experience so humans can see beyond the cloud of fearful ego they have created. Humans' egos are in a cloud, a cloud of mindlessness, powerlessness and hopelessness. Once a human mind falls under the spell of the ego's pull and the influence of this world, it can be difficult to see another way. But there is another way.

This world is indeed a beautiful gift of experience; we just need to awaken to see it as such. If you have awakened, do not give up and fall prey to the lost ego sense of this world. Stay positive, surround yourself with beauty as well as fun, lively, passionate people. Create an oasis for yourself, and when you are given the opportunity, try to inspire, uplift and bring joy to those around you. Those living in the cloud will sense you, see and feel your success in seeing another way. They will be inspired to know what you are doing and thinking. When they have the courage to ask, you can tell them, "I choose to see a different way. I choose to love life."

Higher consciousness is ours to experience because it is the eternal part of who we all are. If we choose, we have the ability to join our own higher conscious awareness with Source—we are not separate. There are many opportunities to awaken our daily conscious thinking to this greater reality while we are physically alive. When awakening occurs, life begins to take on a special meaning. We begin to realize we have the power to create the life we want and have the experiences we wish to experience, while also gaining the courage to be our authentic selves. The knowledge that we are eternally loved by Source replaces the uncertain thoughts of, "Am I enough?" or "Am I being judged by some unseen higher power?"

Having a higher conscious perspective of life brings us the realization that we do not have real enemies in this world, for enemies are created through the illusion of ego beliefs and are not a spiritual reality. In reality, we are all extensions of Source having a physical experience. It is only by seeing life through our ego filters that we believe we are separate, different and against one another. This world is a result of the billions of past and present ego ideas projected upon it, but none of these ego ideas are truly correct if they do not recognize the Source we all are part of.

Having a higher conscious perspective will not change this world, but it will allow us to understand what the world is and to be less affected by the dramas created by ego. This does not mean we turn a blind eye to the wrongdoings of this world. Instead it means we have a sense of a greater reality—a reality in which we stand up to intolerance and hate but also forgive those who are intolerant and hateful because we understand how their minds become influenced by negative ego programming. There will always be a need for one with a higher conscious mind to stand up and fight for freedom and human rights, because in a world where ego dominates and oppresses individual expression, there is a need to stand up and resist the intolerance and hate it brings. Standing up for equality and freedom is also standing up for what is right in the Universe and what is in alignment with our greater Source. There may never truly be peace on Earth, but for those who live life through a higher conscious perspective, there will be inner peace and an understanding of humanity. As a result, the awakened will carry love and joy in their hearts and no ego powers or actions of this world can take away this loving inner connection they have with Source.

It takes sitting alone with ourselves and quieting our endless ego distractions to recognize our greater connection to Source. When we do recognize this connection, we begin the beautiful journey of receiving guidance, intuition, creative inspiration, wisdom and a feeling of being connected to all that is. We also realize we have the power to manifest the life we want because we understand we are all divine, eternal Souls connected to and part of Source. Our Source is the energy of love, and when we strengthen our mental connection to Source we gain what so many have lost in this lifetime: a connection to loving ourselves and loving others.

ᛦExercise: Allowing Source to guide and heal

The following exercises will help you open yourself to receiving energy and insight from Source. Receiving from Source is recognized in various ways by people, but for most it comes through creative thinking and inspiration. You can tell the difference between the higher consciousness of Source and ego because ego likes to judge, command and focus on fear while Source likes to provide wisdom, loving guidance and support.

Source is always bringing us the energy of life, the energy of healing, the energy of knowledge and creative inspiration. It is through our own free will that we awaken and open ourselves to recognizing and receiving it or allow our ego minds to continue ignoring and blocking it.

Go to your sanctuary or a quiet place and allow your mind to be peaceful and quiet. Listen to relaxing non-verbal music, white noise or a fountain if you need to, but do not continue to do anything that may provoke your ego thinking. When you are relaxed you move into a state of higher conscious awareness—this is where you align your mind with Source.

We will use three different methods: **visualization, prayer** and stating **affirmations** in the following exercises to help you mentally connect with Source. You can choose the one you are comfortable with or you may do them all. If you prefer to meditate then you may meditate before or after.

I realize it can be hard to visualize higher consciousness as part of the creative source behind everything. You may prefer to focus on the white light of God, angels, your guides, a loved one who is now in heaven or nature. It does not matter; they are all part of Source. Because they are not part of ego, focusing on them will help align your awareness with higher consciousness. Please do not worry if you connect with Source or not, because through your intentions and by quieting your mind, you will. Even if you do not feel anything different you are still making a connection, which is beneficial.

Receiving Healing from Source

Visualization: Visualize energy from Source as white light coming through your body and emanating from you. Visualize this energy surrounding you in a protective white light. Visualize this white light as penetrating all the cells of your body, bringing them to a higher vibration of health and vitality.

Prayer: "Source, please surround me with healing white light and come fully into my presence. I ask you to bring balanced energy into my body to heal all aspects of myself, my mind, my energetic body and my physical body. I ask that you clean and clear my body of anything that is low vibrational or creating illness."

Affirmation: "The healing energy of Source washes through all the cells of my body, rejuvenating me and healing my body. Through this process I am healed and whole. I am one with my Source, one with my creator. I am healthy and at peace, I am loved, and so it is!"

If you have a specific area of your body that you wish to focus on healing, it is beneficial to add it to your visualization, prayer or affirmation.

Asking Source for Creative Inspiration and Guidance

Keep a notebook or journal nearby to write down anything you feel or sense. If you get an idea, just start writing without judgement. You can go back later and analyze what you wrote and correct any grammar or sentence structure.

Visualization: See yourself surrounded in the white light of Source. Visualize Source bringing wisdom and ideas into your mind. Begin using your imagination and writing down anything that inspires you. *Imagination is connected to Source, so don't worry if you think you are just imagining everything.*

Prayer: "I ask Source to help guide me today and every day. I ask Source to bring divine inspiration and creative ideas to my mind to inspire me to act upon my greatest good. I know the guidance from Source is for the greater good of all and I am open to receive this wisdom."

Affirmation: "I am worthy of receiving inspiration and wisdom from Source. I am one with the creative Source that creates Universes and I am part of this process. I receive divine inspiration and so it is!"

These exercises are examples and are meant to assist you on your journey. Please change the terminology, titles or requests to suit your beliefs. Immediately, or in time, you will receive inspiration, ideas and wisdom. They may not come in the exact moment you ask, instead they may come to you in a sudden inspirational moment. Loving urges may also come through at a later time, such as the simple urge to smile at someone, compliment them or say hello. Other inspiring ideas may come through, perhaps the inspiration to start a business or write a book!

Keep your journal handy when you are doing your spiritual practices, or have mindful moments to write down what comes to your mind. Wisdom, guidance and insight may come during your day-to-day activities so don't dismiss inspirational ideas that suddenly come to mind. If you are busy, try to write a quick note or send yourself a text message to remind you to revisit the idea later. By becoming more aware you strengthen the ability to recognize and receive insightful thoughts as part of your daily routine, bringing a beautiful and loving experience to life.

Living with Higher Consciousness

With practice and patience, we can learn to quiet our ever-persistent ego thoughts and have moments of peaceful awareness. In this peaceful awareness we can sense our divine connection to Source and our connection to all things. This is what it means to travel the path to higher consciousness—a life lived with greater understanding of ourselves and our place in this world. With this awareness we have the courage to be our authentic selves and do the things in this life that truly make us happy and bring us comfort.

When we are being our most authentic and highest versions of ourselves, we see the judgement coming from others as a sign that they are victims of their limited and insecure ego mind, grasping for the meaning in life and fearing everything around them. Our higher conscious awareness will lead us to have compassion for those who cannot see beyond their ego thoughts, but we do not need to participate in the ever-present drama they create. They see us when we are living authentically and happily and will perhaps be inspired to awaken their own minds to a greater reality. If they begin to seek, we can lovingly help them see a better way. If they do not, it's OK; we are all on our own journeys and we can peacefully move on.

Source does not love the awakened more than those who are asleep and under the spell of ego; Source loves us all the same. The difference is that those who have awakened realize they can create their own heaven on Earth. Living in a higher conscious state of mind means we know we are always a beloved part of Source and we can live this Earthy life as fabulously as we choose. When we become positively aligned with Source, we experience the harmonious flow of all our dreams coming into existence.

Living in a higher conscious state of mind creates a reality in which receiving guidance, inspiration, knowledge and creative ideas becomes our normal. Through this state of mind, we experience a fast-track to having all that we desire in this earthly life, not because we are chosen over others, but rather because we have chosen to quiet our minds and listen. We chose to awaken and know we are a beloved part of Source and to allow ourselves to experience our connection to Source while we are alive in our physical bodies.

Living in a higher conscious state of mind is higher living, a life of more abundance, success, peace and happiness. Awaken your mind, love yourself and connect with Source—the world is yours to create. Go create with passion and Source will be your ever-present creative companion.

Source senses your energy as vibration and light and when you are in a positive, receptive state, your light shines

BRIGHTER.

Acknowledgements

Thank you to my husband for reading over my original writings and helping me get my ideas into a cohesive book.

A special thanks to my friend Stephanie Toczynski for being the first to do the exercises and for giving me insightful feedback. I hope you're enjoying the process of manifesting—from the looks of it, you are!

Thank you to my development editor and book coach, Heather Doyle Fraser from Beyond Change, LLC for giving me excellent insight in bringing my ideas and exercises all together, and also for the many helpful tips to bring this book to fruition.

Thank you Jessica Lowman of Jessica Lowman Photography, for my headshots and assistance with book design.

And of course, thank you to Source for providing me the wisdom, courage and insight to write this book and the patience to get it completed.

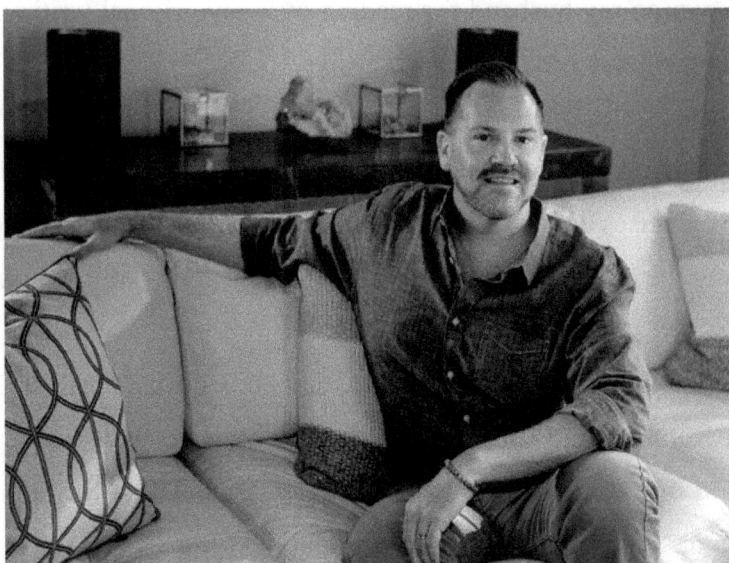

About the Author

David Howard, PhD, is a Metaphysical Guide and owner of Transcendent Lifestyle LLC, which offers guidance through metaphysical concepts and meditation to help people transform their lives. He received his ministerial doctorate from the University of Sedona and his masters from The University of Metaphysics, and continues his research into connecting with Source. He is not your typical minister. Dr. Howard teaches about how we can be our most authentic selves and live every day in a way that is fun and feels good. He does not believe anyone needs to conform or change who they truly are to be on a spiritual path, instead spirituality should complement who they are and their lifestyle. His ultimate goal is to show how spirituality can complement the modern man and woman by helping them find success and happiness in a hectic and sometimes chaotic world.

David lives with his husband in Powell, Ohio and enjoys being surrounded by nature, entertaining friends and celebrating life. He is free spirited, fun loving, compassionate to others and passionate about helping people find joy and meaning in their lives. You can learn more about and what he does on his website www.transcendentlifestyle.com.